**A STUDY GUIDE
COMMENTARY**

HOSEA

HOSEA

A STUDY GUIDE
COMMENTARY

D. DAVID GARLAND

ZONDERVAN
PUBLISHING HOUSE

OF THE ZONDERVAN CORPORATION
GRAND RAPIDS, MICHIGAN 49506

To
LARRY and JANE
on the occasion of their marriage
and to
DAVID MARSHALL
upon his graduation

HOSEA: A STUDY GUIDE

© 1975 by The Zondervan Corporation
Grand Rapids, Michigan

Library of Congress Catalog Card Number 75-6180

Printed in the United States of America

CONTENTS

PREFACE

This study represents an attempt to provide a brief volume dealing with the main themes reflected in the book of Hosea. It is not a critical study. It was written to be read along with the Bible.

To gain the most from this volume, the student should first read the scripture references in the section headings and then read the materials included here which attempt to explain what has been read.

This effort does not pretend to be exhaustive. It deals broadly with the great themes of the book, and the prophet's way of dealing with them.

I am indebted to Zondervan for requesting the manuscript, my teachers for an interest in the prophets, my colleagues and Mrs. Velma Brown, who read the manuscript, the Administration of Southwestern Baptist Theological Seminary for their assistance, and Miss Charlotte Jones for typing the manuscript.

D. DAVID GARLAND

Southwestern Baptist Theological Seminary
Fort Worth, Texas 76122

CHAPTER 1

INTRODUCING THE PROPHET

Hosea appears first among the minor prophets of the Old Testament. Though first in order, the book is not considered to have been the earliest of the group. That distinction belongs to Amos. Hosea is generally believed to have been a later contemporary of Amos, as will be seen in the subsequent discussions.

1. *The Personal History of Hosea.* Information concerning the personal life and history of Hosea is meager. He was known as the son of Beeri (1:1). There have been attempts to identify Beeri as a prince of Reuben taken captive to Assyria by Tiglath-Pileser during the reign of Pekah (737-732 B.C.) (1 Chron. 5:6; 2 Kings 15:29). Efforts have been made, also, to associate him with the village of Belemoth or Belemon of the tribe of Issachar, but neither of these attempts has met with success.

Hosea's name means "salvation." Whether this is a reflection of the faith of Hosea's father is unknown. Yet it may have been a statement of the father's belief that his son would play a role in Israel's future salvation. Or it could have implied the continuation of his own household. At any rate the name of Hosea is identical with that of Joshua, the successor to Moses (Num. 13:8, 16), and Hoshea, the last king of Israel (2 Kings 18:1).

Hosea was married to Gomer, the daughter of Diblaim, an otherwise unknown citizen from an unknown family of Northern Israel. She bore him three children. The circumstances of the marriage have provoked voluminous discussions as to its nature and character.

In stating the circumstances of God's initial dealings with him, Hosea related that he was commanded to take to wife a woman of "whoredoms." These instructions from God raised a serious moral

9

problem for the prophet, however, because he was strongly opposed in his preaching to a similar moral decadence found throughout the nation and reflected in the disappearance of virtue and honor from the society of Israel.

The problem of the marriage has been approached in three basic ways. The older commentators interpreted the marriage allegorically. They taught that there was no actual marriage between the prophet and Gomer. The purpose of the whole story was to illustrate the relationship between Israel and Yahweh. Yet, to have the prophet say that God began to deal with him first through his marriage would raise serious objections to an allegorical approach. Evidently the prophet was talking about his own marriage, not a make-believe one. Too, the name Gomer does not necessarily reflect a symbolic meaning. For these reasons, if for no others, the allegorical interpretation would be open to question.

A second group of commentators has taken a literal approach to the problem. They simply state that God commanded the prophet to marry an immoral woman, that is, a harlot. The objection to this position is in the fact that the word characterizing Gomer and her activity is the same as that used to characterize the activity of Israel. When used to describe the activity of Israel, "whoredom" refers to idolatry rather than harlotry. Though harlotry may be implicit in "whoredoms," it may not refer to the act of immorality as such. Therefore, it would not necessarily follow that Gomer was a harlot. At most it would reflect the possibility of idolatry, not adultery. The term for "whoredom" is a plural form, and that in itself may suggest idolatry. Also, the term for adultery is an entirely different word from that used for whoredom. Another objection is that an adulteress, such as Gomer was supposed to be, would have been stoned to death by the people of her community. She certainly would not have been a fitting wife for a prophet. In light of these considerations, plus the moral problem created for the prophet by such a command, the literal approach is open to serious question.

A third approach to the nature of the marriage, though it does not eliminate every problem, is to consider the possibility that Gomer was a virtuous woman at the time of her marriage, but one with idolatrous tendencies. After her marriage to Hosea, however, she turned to the Baalim. In doing so, she followed the practice of idolatry which ultimately led her into temple prostitution (adultery) and at last into slavery, where she is found in chapter 3.

Thus, Hosea looked back across the years, after much or even most of his ministry to Israel, and as he did, he saw that God's initial preparation of him for his role was in his marriage to Gomer which brought such shame upon his home and such personal pain to himself. In fact, he saw Israel's faithlessness to God — beginning with idolatry which led to adultery — as a counterpart to his own tragic experience with Gomer, who turned first to idols and then to adultery.

Though the above explanation does not resolve every aspect of the problem, it may leave fewer difficulties than some of the others which have been considered. The matter will be extended and expanded in chapter 2.

2. *The Date of Hosea's Ministry.* On the basis of the references to Jeroboam the king of Israel, and Uzziah, Jotham, Ahaz, and Hezekiah, kings of Judah, the outside limits for the ministry of Hosea would range somewhere between 786 B.C., the beginning year of Jeroboam's reign, and 686 B.C., the concluding year of Hezekiah's reign.

There are, however, narrower limits to the length of his ministry. The first is that Israel was destroyed by the Assyrians in 722 B.C. Therefore, Hosea would have of necessity carried out his mission prior to that date. A second evidence related to the prophet's date is reflected in Hosea's reference to Gilead, Galilee and Naphtali. They were considered to be a part of Israel. Yet, 2 Kings 15:29 states that the population of these areas had been deported to Assyria in 734 B.C. Therefore, Hosea's ministry must have been prior to 734 B.C.

As to the beginning of Hosea's ministry, the first three chapters show the prosperous conditions which were also reflected in the ministry of Amos, about 750 B.C. Therefore, the probable dates for Hosea would be between 750-734 B.C., and certainly no later than the fall of the Northern Kingdom in 722 B.C.

3. *The Occupation of the Prophet.* It has been suggested that prior to the beginning of his prophetic ministry, Hosea may have been engaged in any one of three occupations.

On the basis of such references as Hosea 4:6; 8:12; 9:3; 9:8; and 9:10, there are those who suggest that Hosea was a priest prior to assuming the role of prophet. His references to the law (4:6 and 8:12), his mention of the clean and unclean (9:3, 10), and his allusion to the Temple persecution (9:8) would lend support to such an hypothesis. Yet others believe Hosea to have been a farmer. His knowledge of wild beasts (5:14; 11:10), his seeming acquaintance with the life of the country (10:11-12), and his frequent references to fig trees would seem to give support to such a theory. As a third possibility, some have suggested that Hosea may have even been a baker (see 7:4).

The most impressive evidence, however, seems to favor his being a farmer. Still, there is nothing to eliminate the possibility that he engaged in more than one of these occupations prior to becoming a prophet. Nevertheless, our main interest is not in what he did prior to his responding to Yahweh's call to be a prophet. Our interest is in what he did as a prophet.

4. *The Times of Hosea.* The times of Hosea were essentially the same as those of his senior colleague, Amos, who had prophesied to Israel during the same general period, though a little earlier.

For fifty years, from approximately the beginning of the eighth century until midway through it, Israel was relatively free from outside interference by nations long opposed to her.

The first of these external enemies to go, a longstanding one at that, was Syria. Syria had provided a threat from the days of Jehu (842-815 B.C.), but she was finally overthrown by the Assyrians during the reign of Adad-Nirari III (811-783 B.C.).

Syria's conquerors, the Assyrians, were next to go. Following their victory over the Syrians, Assyria began to decline. That removed her as a challenge to Israel, so that the nation was no longer threatened by this once powerful enemy. At the same time Egypt was weakened by internal dissension and disorganization. So, for one of the very few times in her history, Israel was relatively free from outside interference.

All of these circumstances, converging upon one time in Israel's history, provided her an unparalleled opportunity to secure herself politically in that part of the world, and to develop economically. Both factors enabled her to reach her second most prosperous era — a period exceeded only by that of the time of David.

One would have expected these new circumstances to have transformed the whole of the society of Israel as well at that of her sister nation, Judah. Just the opposite was the case, however. During these years the middle class had disappeared. The balance which this group provides to any society was now lost. As is always the case when this happens, Israel was left with two classes, the rich and the poor. The rich grew richer and poor grew poorer. Injustice became widespread as the rich gained the upper hand and took advantage of the less fortunate in every area of society.

In addition to the new independence and the economic expansion of the period, there was a resurgence of religious activity. The people adopted religious customs foreign to the traditions of Israel, through which the religious leadership lost its sense of values as well as its direction. Though religious activity increased, it was the wrong kind. It was mere pretense.

Such times called for a man who understood the pain of betrayal. One knowing the heartbreak of disappointment in his own experience would best serve God's purpose for such a time. Certainly no man had suffered more than had Hosea, as a result of Gomer's disloyalty, and no man knew more about the grace required in taking her back. Because of his own background, Yahweh chose Hosea for such a time.

5. *Hosea the Man.* Unlike Amos, the rustic preacher of judgment, Hosea was a gentle, loving spirit. He has been referred to as "the tenderest soul of all the prophets." Though severe in his denunciation of sin, he was compassionate in his attitude toward men — an attitude no doubt learned in the tragedy of his own home. These attitudes were reflected in every aspect of the prophet's life. They are seen first in his family relations (1:2 to 3:5). The tragedy of Hosea's marriage to Gomer must have cast a shadow over his entire ministry. An ordinary man would have put such an unfaithful wife away for life, but not Hosea. His love for her was so genuine it could withstand years of profligacy. This devotion to Gomer is seen in his willingness, yea, desire, to take her back and make her his wife again. Few men love like that or have such a capacity to forgive and restore.

It could be that Hosea's greatest contribution to the world was his commitment to his wife and family. Though no one could condone Gomer's conduct, who is the man who would condemn the compassion of the prophet in forgiving her and rebuilding a home around her!

Hosea's compassionate spirit expressed itself in his attitude toward the sins of the nation (2:2-23). In this section the prophet expressed a concern for his own people, who had been as unfaithful to Yahweh as Gomer had been to him. He saw Yahweh wooing them through tender words of love and mercy, believing all the while that these words would eventually touch the heart of his people. They, as a result, did turn to Yahweh and declare him to be their God.

Though a man of compassion and love, Hosea was severe in his condemnation of sin. He saw that the nation was at times totally lacking in truth and goodness and a knowledge of God (4:1). This was a nation of commandment-breakers who deserved nothing but the destructive storms of Yahweh's wrath (4:2-19).

In large measure, Hosea blamed the leaders for Israel's predicament (5:1-15). Yet, he joined heart with Yahweh when God determined to destroy them all, but could not (11:8). Hosea felt the heartbeat of God, and realized He would find a way to restore fallen Israel, and He would do it out of a compassionate heart.

Hosea believed that Yahweh would, after judging the nation, return to bless them. He would be their source of healing and life if they would turn to Him. It was a merciful God whom the prophet served. To serve such a God meant that the servant must be like the one he served. Few men succeeded in that noble aspiration as did Hosea, and few have left such a legacy.

How different any generation would be if it could find a balance between judgment and mercy, as the prophet did. It would, indeed, make a lasting difference.

FOR FURTHER STUDY

1. For a discussion of the conditions in Israel at the time of Hosea read pp. 249-262 in *A History of Israel*, second edition, by John Bright.
2. Read the article on "Hosea (Man and Book)" in *The Interpreter's Dictionary of the Bible*, Volume II, pp. 648-653 or *The Zondervan Pictorial Bible Dictionary*, p. 861. (From this point on the *Interpreter's Dictionary of the Bible* will be referred to as IDB and *The Zondervan Pictorial Bible Dictionary* as ZPBD).
3. Read the articles on "Prostitution" in IDB, Volume III, pp. 931-934 and "Whore" in ZPBD, p. 893.
4. After a careful study of the conditions in Israel at the time of Hosea's ministry, which of these do you find in your own society? How are these manifest? In light of the lessons of history what do they portend in your judgment?
5. What can you do to help correct those conditions which are harmful to you and your community?

CHAPTER 2

FROM TRAGEDY TO TRIUMPH
(1:2-2:1)

1. The Beginning of Yahweh's Speaking (1:2*a*)
2. The Ultimate Purpose of Hosea's Experience (1:2*b*)
3. The Resultant Marriage (1:3*a*)
4. The Birth of Hosea's Son (1:3*b*-5)
5. The Children of Gomer's Profligacy (1:6-9)
6. The Day of Jezreel — a Day of Triumph (1:10-2:1)

The events described in this section of Hosea reflect, in a broader sense, the tragic conditions existing in Israel and Judah at the time of the prophet's ministry. That is, the domestic tragedy in Hosea's home was a miniature of a far greater tragedy in the nations. That tragedy was in their having turned from Yahweh to other gods. Such turning could only result in God's displeasure and their own destruction.

Even though God's displeasure suggested the destruction of the nation(s), a not-to-be-forgotten sovereign purpose was involved in Yahweh's dealings with the offspring of Abraham. The realization of that purpose depended, ultimately, upon the character and nature of God. (It was, of course, dependent to a lesser degree upon the attitude and conduct of the people.) Yahweh could turn the present tragedy, expressed in the nation's rebelliousness and idolatry, into triumph; this He would do in "the day of Jezreel." This section of Hosea relates the events leading toward that day.

1. *The Beginning of Yahweh's Speaking* (1:2*a*). When his prophecies were being compiled, Hosea reflected back across the difficult years of his ministry. He decided that his marriage to Gomer was the beginning of Yahweh's dealings with him. He saw Yahweh communicating to him, in his marriage to Gomer, truths which he could never really understand apart from personal knowledge. Therefore, his heartbreaking experience in his own home was of primary significance in his preparation for the task Yahweh had for him. In fact, Hosea saw this as the initial stage in that preparation, and said so (1:2*a*).

15

Hosea's marriage to Gomer raises certain moral and ethical issues which cannot be easily resolved. Many question whether Yahweh would have directed, or even allowed, one of his prophets to marry an immoral woman. Whatever else may be said about this matter, it is out of character for God to do so. Even so, some contend this is precisely what God did.

This contention has been challenged by substantial objections. The first is that the purpose of Hosea's marriage was to show a parallel between this relationship and that existing between Yahweh and Israel. If so, and Hosea did indeed marry an immoral woman, the analogy is lost because Hosea stated that the evil in Israel developed after "their" marriage, when they became as abominable as the things which they loved (9:10).

A second objection is found in the unlikely prospect that a prophet of such high moral standards would be commanded by Yahweh to marry an immoral woman. Also, had this been the will of Yahweh for Hosea, it is more likely that the term "whoredoms" would not have been strong enough to characterize an unchaste woman. The term for such a person would have been "harlot" — a much stronger term. "Whoredoms" is a term used most frequently to characterize one guilty of idolatry, not adultery.

These objections, and others which could be suggested, raise a serious question as to whether God did indeed command Hosea to marry an immoral woman.

Some have attempted to remove the moral difficulty of Hosea's marriage by interpreting the whole account as an allegory. Now, an allegory is a description of one thing under the image of another. That is, one thing symbolizes or stands for another. This approach is objected to on the grounds that the usual symbolism found in an allegory is lacking. For example, no known symbolic significance seems to be given to the name of Hosea's wife. Had the account been an allegory, there would have been some significance to the name. The allegorical approach is also objected to on the grounds that the moral problem is no more resolved by this approach than by the former ones.

A third approach, though not taking care of all of the problems, does eliminate some of the objections raised to the other theories. This approach suggests that Hosea married an idolatrous woman, who, after the marriage and the birth of the first child, went off into adultery. Though this explanation does not remove the problem of a prophet's marrying an idolatrous woman, it does not leave him with the formidable problem of adultery and the real probability of Gomer's being stoned to death. In the case of idolatry, there is always the possibility of a person's being led back from the way which, if pursued, could lead to adultery and ultimately to death.

This third approach has the advantage of providing a definite parallel. That is, Israel's first great sin was idolatry — a sin which led to an accentuation of the sensual, which led to immorality. This theory also provides a means of reconciling Hosea's denunciation of sexual immorality and his marriage to one who had idolatrous tendencies. Finally, it provides the best explanation of the progressive deterioration of Gomer's character. This is seemingly reflected in the record of Gomer's children. It is definitely stated that the first child was Hosea's. This seems to suggest, at least, the possibility that the other two were born to Gomer, but not by Hosea. If this was the case, it is possible to see the decline of Gomer to idolatry and, at last, to adultery. And this decline was paralleled in the history of the relationship between Yahweh and Israel. Though not removing all of the problems, this last approach carries the best basis of analogy and the fewest unresolved problems.

2. *The Ultimate Purpose of Hosea's Experience* (1:2b). The primary reason for Hosea's marriage to Gomer, as he later came to see, was not to fulfill love, though it was that, nor to establish a home, while it was that, nor to bring offspring into the world, and it did that. The major purpose was to enable the prophet to understand the nature of the relationship between Yahweh and Israel. This understanding, gained from a firsthand knowledge of unfaithfulness, would make Hosea a more effective prophet to the nation. For Israel was equally unfaithful in its relationship to Yahweh. In other words, the tragedy of Hosea's domestic life was a miniature of a larger tragedy in the Yahweh-Israel relationship. Knowing the heartache of his own experience, Hosea could better understand Yahweh's disappointment over Israel's unfaithfulness since God's experience was so similar to that of the prophet.

It has been well said that experience is life's greatest teacher. If the claim allows for one's experience to include the divine-human encounter, or at least a knowledge of it, this is truly an accurate statement. In the divine-human encounter the real potential of experience is most likely to be realized. That potential is not just in what an individual learns. It is in what others can be taught from these experiences. This was the case with Hosea. His experience enabled him to teach others so that they might escape the suffering he had had to endure.

17

3. *The Resultant Marriage* (1:3*a*). In keeping with what he believed to be the providential purpose of Yahweh, Hosea married Gomer, the daughter of Diblaim. Her name means "completeness." Some have interpreted this to mean "consummation," "daughter of double fig-cake," or even, "utter ruin." These terms, it is generally held, all refer to Gomer's wicked activity or to her lust.

Diblaim, the name of Gomer's father, means a "double lump of figs." It has been suggested that this name could have been a figure for sweetness. Combined with Gomer, some contend it may have meant that Israel, having forsaken Yahweh, had found its sweetness in the pleasures which corrupt. Or, if this were a reference to Gomer, it may have meant that she could be bought at the market of profligacy for two figs or, perhaps, for two fig cakes.

On the other hand, there are those who would disallow any of the prior explanations regarding the names. They would insist that every effort to find any symbolism in the names is futile, and they may well be correct. If they are, then the names are to be taken as no more than names, and all attempts at symbolism are to be ignored.

4. *The Birth of Hosea's Son* (1:3*b*-5). Some time after the marriage (and the length of time is not specified) Gomer "bore him a son" (1:3*b*). The "him" should be taken as a reference to Hosea as the father. In light of the specific reference here and its absence in 1:6 and 1:8, many hold that the first child, Jezreel, was the only one of the three children fathered by Hosea. This suggestion has merit. It seems to follow the supposition of the third theory dealing with the marriage discussed earlier. In that case, the first child would have been born prior to Gomer's profligacy. He indeed would have been the son of Hosea, as reflected in the words, "bore him a son." The absence of the word "him" in the announcement of the other children raises a question as to their paternity. This matter will be considered in the discussion of 1:6-9, however.

The son born to Hosea was named Jezreel, as Yahweh had instructed. In this case, as in so many but not in all others, the name seems to have had a special significance. It means "God sows." It was, no doubt, a reference to the valley where Gideon resoundingly defeated the Midianites (Judg. 6-7) or to the town of Jezreel, from whence the valley supposedly received its name. The name has possibly a twofold implication. First, it refers back to the disastrous destruction of the house of Ahab by Jehu (2 Kings 9-10); and second, it points forward to the judgment yet to come upon the dynasty of Jehu for having destroyed the house of Ahab, now identified as Israel, the Northern Kingdom. The judgment to fall upon "the house of Jehu" for the "blood of Jezreel," was Yahweh's judgment upon Jehu for the bloody slaughter of Ahab's house at Jezreel. This had evidently been too severe, and had placed Jehu's house under a judgment which was imminent. It would come in "yet a little while."

Though the realization of this judgment was delayed somewhat, it did supposedly come to pass in the murder of Zachariah by Shallum (2 Kings 15:10), and in the fall of the Northern Kingdom in 722 B.C. (2 Kings 17). In the latter case, the bow (a metaphor for military might) of Israel was broken in the fall of Samaria before the onslaught of the Assyrians, and in that event the judgment upon Jehu was at last realized.

5. *The Children of Gomer's Profligacy* (1:6-9). After the account of the birth of the first child, Jezreel, and the subsequent judgment, there follow the accounts of the birth of two other children to Gomer. The second to be born was Lo-ruhamah, a daughter.

The report of the birth of Lo-ruhamah is quite different from that of Jezreel. In the earlier account, the narrative states that Gomer conceived and bore Hosea a son. Though scholars do not agree on the significance of the words, it stands to reason that they may well indicate that Jezreel was without question the offspring of Hosea and Gomer. In the case of Lo-ruhamah, on the other hand, the words concerning Hosea's paternity are lacking. It seems most likely that their absence was for the purpose of suggesting that the child conceived by Gomer was not, in fact, the child of Hosea. She may well have been the offspring of Gomer's profligacy, conceived perhaps in her activity as a temple prostitute, if she did indeed become such.

The very name given this child seems to weigh in favor of her not being fathered by Hosea. For the gentle Hosea to have named his own child Lo-ruhamah ("unpitied") seems most unlikely. On the other hand, if the child was not his, the name would have reflected the theological thinking of the time. That is, the name would have reflected the belief that the sins of the fathers (mothers, in this case) would be visited upon the children, and the child's not knowing compassion would be prophetic of Israel's not knowing Yahweh's compassion.

If then the circumstances of Hosea's home was a miniature of what was happening in the broader context to the nation, the account was simply stating that the compassion and forgiveness which Israel had known on former occasions were to be no longer available. The people, like the child of Gomer, were no longer deserving of favor. Israel, then, would find herself subject to the judgment of God (1:6). She would find herself in a state in which pity was lacking.

19

Judah, on the other hand, would know the compassion of Yahweh (1:7). It would not be realized by the usual means, "by bow, nor by sword, nor by battle, by horses, nor by horsemen." God's compassion would be seen in His personal intervention as when He delivered Jerusalem from Sennacherib in 701 B.C. (See 2 Kings 19:32-34.) In fact, it may have been that very event which the prophet had in mind.

In whatever way one may interpret the details of the above reference, the point is there was a difference in the character of Israel and Judah at that particular time. Israel, filled with wickedness and injustice, would be denied Yahweh's pity. Judah, on the other hand, would experience His remarkable power and compassion in deliverance (1:7a).

The birth of the next child follows the same general pattern as that of the second. After the weaning of Lo-ruhamah, Gomer conceived and bore a third child, who was named Lo-ammi (1:8).

The name of the last child no doubt reflected the attitude of the prophet toward it. It means "not my people." Hence, by giving the child such a name, the prophet was disallowing his own paternity; he was declaring it to be the offspring of another. As in the previous case, the experience of Hosea was a symbol of the relationship between Yahweh and Israel. Israel, because of her relationship with and devotion to other deities, was no more Yahweh's than Lo-ammi was Hosea's. Thus, verse 9 comes to the heart of the tragic condition in Hosea's family and, ultimately, to the larger tragedy relating to the nation. In light of the existing conditions within Israel, they were no longer considered to be Yahweh's covenant people. By their actions they had broken the covenant. As a result, Yahweh would no longer be I AM (literally, "I will be") for them. What a tragic turn of events! Those who had once been Yahweh's ("my people") would no longer be His, and the one who had been their God would no longer be so.

If our interpretation of this section is a viable one, and it seems to be, then the following is the picture presented by the prophet. At first, Gomer was a faithful wife who bore Hosea a son. This son was given the name Jezreel. As time passed Gomer gave in to the claims of idolatry and may have, as some believe, degenerated into a temple prostitute. During the time she was involved in this degrading activity, Gomer gave birth to her second and third children. Neither of these was specifically referred to as being Hosea's. On this account, it has been assumed that the names given them reflected the belief of Hosea that they were born to Gomer by someone other than himself. By analogy, these names reflected God's attitude toward the offspring of Israel who had resulted from the idolatrous relations between the nation and their pagan deities. Those born to Israel were not Yahweh's; they were the children of other gods.

6. *The Day of Jezreel – a Day of Triumph* (1:10-2:1). This paragraph (1:10 to 2:1), in sharp contrast with its context, has been questioned by scholars through the years. They have contended that the passive nature of verse 10 and the concept of the reunion of the divided house of Israel reflect an approach less Hosea's than the context would demand. Some have even suggested that this concept was exilic and should, therefore, be denied Hosea.

In addition to the problems of nature and approach, it has been argued that the problem of context may be resolved more easily by placing these verses after either 2:23 or 3:5. In either case, the contention is based upon what is believed to be a more favorable context. That is, 2:23 and 3:5 both deal with hope and promise. Therefore, they provide a better atmosphere for the good days promised in 1:10-2:1.

On the other hand, 1:10 2:1 may be simply following the pattern consistent with most prophets. They often alternated between words of hope and promise, and words of condemnation and judgment. If such were the case, there would seem to be little reason for questioning the construction or the context of the section. In that case, the words may be attributed to the prophet, in keeping with an established pattern, as words depicting the ultimate triumph of Yahweh's purpose in Israel (and Judah).

This section opens with an idealized promise concerning the future. Israel would be as numerous as the sands of the sea. This was not a new idea. It was the reiteration of an idea of long standing and anticipated for generations — from the time of Abraham, as a matter of fact.

This promise was, nevertheless, very meaningful at this particular point in Israel's history. First, the population of Israel had lost ground through the years (cf. 2 Kings 15:19ff.); second, Israel's future looked dark because of Assyria's position as a superior power. On account of these things, more than any others, Israel's future was under a cloud. The need for a word of encouragement was obvious. These words were, in part at least, a response to that need. They were, also, words of abiding worth to sustain the people as they faced their enemies and suffered one loss after another. How consoling it must have been for them to hear Yahweh's announcement that the population of the nation would be greatly expanded in the future.

In addition to the promise of a greatly expanded population, there was a promise of covenant renewal. Those who had been referred to as "not my people" — that is, those who gave allegiance to other deities — would come to be called "sons of the living God." The latter part of verse 10 is not to be looked upon as a result of the expansion of the population. Just the opposite is the case. The renewal of the covenant would be the ground of the population increase. The future development of Israel rested upon the reestablishment of a proper relationship between Yahweh and His people.

A third promise follows in verse 11a. Here is held out the possibility of the reunion of Israel and Judah, a thing constantly hoped for since the tragic division in 922 B.C. What bright prospects were to be associated with that event! How glorious the day would be when peace and unity once more prevailed. It was too good to be true. Nothing short of a miracle could bring it to pass. Since a miracle would be required, it became identified with the messianic age, which was related to the miraculous glories of the future.

An additional promise found in this section is the concept of "one head." The united Israel would have "one head" (one ruler). That "one head" would be able to bring about a change in the attitude of Israel toward Judah, and vice versa. The new king would be the unifying force which would lead the nation to reestablish itself as in the days of David. When that time arrived, the nation which had been carried into exile, would "go up from the land." They would go up from exile, repossess their land, and become the great nation which they had been during David's reign.

In this case, as in the former, there is nothing against the idea that these events were to be realized in the messianic age. If, indeed, this was Hosea's thinking, he may have equated all of these accomplishments with the messianic age. He also equated the messianic age with the reign of the second David. Hosea believed that when that reign was finally established, all of the promises made by Yahweh in the days of Israel's trouble would be realized. What a day it would be! It would be the day of Jezreel! It would be a day of victory — a day when Israel would triumph over those who had defeated them earlier in the plains of Jezreel. This new day of Jezreel, no doubt another aspect of the messianic hope, would see the land sown with the innumerable hosts of Israel. The age to come would have been established. It would indeed be "the day of Jezreel," because Yahweh would have (re)sown the land with those who had been denied it by their enemies. They would once again be His people, the recipients of His mercy (2:11).

Thus we have seen the prophet's method of dealing with Israel's current state and, at the same time, his means of extending hope. He pointed to the tragic road before the nation, but not solely to the darkness of the way. He pointed beyond it to something better. He saw the road leading from tragedy to triumph, but the triumph would be the work of Yahweh. And the work of Yahweh would be accomplished in the messianic age by the Messiah Himself. What a triumph that would be!

FOR FURTHER STUDY

1. What difficulties, if any, do you find with the supposition that Hosea was instructed by Yahweh to marry a harlot? How do you personally resolve the problem? Why do you reject the other suggested solutions?
2. Read the articles on "Jezreel" in IDB, Volume II, pp. 906-907 and in ZPBD, p. 432.
3. Read the articles on "Jehu" in IDB, Volume II, pp. 817-819 and in ZPBD, pp. 408-409.
4. Do you believe the specific reference to Jezreel's being the child of Hosea and the omission of the reference in the case of the other children reflect the real situation in the family life of the prophet? If not, why not? Discuss.
5. Were conditions in Judah vastly different from those in Israel at the time of Hosea? If not, how do you explain the favorable attitude reflected toward Judah in the book of Hosea? Discuss.
6. Read the articles on "Sennacherib" in IDB, Volume IV, pp. 270-272 and in ZPBD, pp. 769-770.
7. Show how the promises of 1:10-2:1 relate to the messianic hope, if you believe them to be so related. If you reject the idea, then to what do you relate them? Discuss.

CHAPTER 3

GOD'S ENDLESS QUEST
(Hosea 2:2-23)

1. Israel's Unfaithfulness (2:2c, 5a, 5b, 8, 13*b*)
2. Yahweh's First Reaction to Israel's Profligacy (2:2a, 2b, 3, 4, 9)
3. Yahweh's Ultimate Response to Israel's Shame (2:6, 7a, 10, 11, 14, 15a)
4. The Effects of Yahweh's Reaction and Response Upon Israel (2:7, 15b, 16-23)

Chapter 2 reflects the moral and religious conditions in Israel around 750 B.C. It also describes the effect these conditions had upon Yahweh and the ways in which Yahweh's reaction affected the nation.

The material in this section is presented as if it were a court trial in which Israel's unfaithfulness becomes the basis of the charges brought against her. At issue was the covenant relationship, which was treated as a covenant of marriage. The wife (Israel, in this case) had broken that covenant in turning from her husband (Yahweh) to follow other lovers (gods) who had now won her affections. By doing so, she had broken the marriage (covenant) relationship.

Contrary to ordinary procedure in such cases, however, there does not follow a description of the judgment deserved, but a command to the children (individual Israelites) to entreat their mother (Israel) to return to her first love (Yahweh). If she would heed their entreaty, the former relationship would be restored, and she would again become the recipient of Yahweh's good pleasure. It was not, as was usually the case, a lawsuit in which a divorce was sought, but a suit in which reconciliation was the goal. The nation, if reconciled to Yahweh, would be restored to her former position and would become the beneficiary of untold spiritual and material blessings from the one whom she had earlier rejected.

This portion of Hosea reflects the unhappy relationship which existed between Gomer and Hosea — a miniature of the larger relationship existing between Yahweh and Israel. It also reflects Yahweh's willingness, as well as His earnest effort, to regain the affection of His wayward bride (Israel). Also, it establishes a context for Hosea's purchase of his own disenchanted mate, which will be discussed in our consideration of Hosea 3.

1. *Israel's Unfaithfulness* (2:2c, 5a, 5b, 8, 13b). The parallel between Hosea's situation and that which existed between Yahweh and Israel is obvious. Like Gomer, Israel had become an unfaithful wife. Her unfaithfulness expressed itself in numerous ways, but primarily in idolatry. The mother (Israel) of the individual Israelites was entreated by her children to turn from her compromising activity of following the Baalim. She was, in fact, entreated not only to refrain from compromising activity, but also to remove every indication of such a way of life (2:2b).

Such removal would have involved all jewelry, or any other adornments worn by the worshipers of Baal — adornments which would instantly identify one as a moral profligate in the eyes of God. If, on the other hand, it was not a reference to jewelry or adornments, it may have been an effort to get Israel to forsake every possible evidence of profligacy. In either case, the call was to forsake every practice compromising the nation's relationship with Yahweh.

The unfaithfulness of Israel was further characterized as harlotry in Hosea. This tragic practice was reflected in Israel's looking to the Baalim as the sources of her bread, water, wool and flax for clothing, and drinks. In each case, these have been primarily referred to as luxury items. That is, the people not only attributed to the Baalim the provision of the needs of life; they also credited these false gods with the luxuries of life (2:5).

To have done this was bad enough in itself. The other side of this tragedy, however, may be seen in verse 8. All the while Israel was attributing their resources to Baal, they were unintentionally, no doubt, denying that Yahweh had been the source of anything. That was, in a way, an act of denial or rejection which but compounded the tragedy of their lives. And, as if that were not enough, they had taken silver and gold, provided by Yahweh, to use in the worship of the Baalim. Whether these precious metals were used to embellish the splendor of the worship of the Baalim or to mold images of the Baalim is not clear. In either case, they were using resources provided by Yahweh, not as acknowledged gifts of His goodness, but as resources to be used in the worship of the Baalim. That was the rankest of heresies.

You may have noticed by now that the last clause of verse 8 uses the singular form for Baal instead of the usual plural form — Baalim. This change has caused many interpreters to reject these words, considering them to be a gloss. Even so — and a difficulty must be acknowledged — the singular does not necessarily exclude the possibility of its being used in a collective sense. If so, this would resolve that particular problem.

In the latter part of 2:13, we find an added statement of Israel's unfaithfulness to Yahweh. They were charged with having burned incense to the Baalim. This was a reference to the Baal cultic activity which the Israelites had adopted. The participants, bedecked, no doubt, in resplendent cultic attire, became so infatuated by the cultic pursuit of their lovers, the Baalim, and the attendant immoralities, that it finally crowded out all memory of Yahweh.

If, indeed, and it is a valid position to hold, the Israelites were trying to equate the worship of Yahweh and Baal, their acknowledged forgetting of Yahweh simply points up the futility, as well as the folly, of such an attempt. Yahweh will not share His place with another. One of the best indications that it cannot be done is seen in this passage. When men attempt it, they inevitably forget the true God; and He, in turn, considers forsaking them. This consideration now becomes the focus of Hosea's attention.

2. *Yahweh's First Reaction to Israel's Profligacy* (2:2b, 3, 4, 9). From the very outset of the court scene (2:2a), Yahweh's impulse had been to disown the offending nation as His wife and to disallow Himself as her husband (2:2b). This would be considered the normal and natural reaction of most husbands. No man could be expected to share his "companion" with another. Therefore, when a woman was known to be guilty of forsaking her mate, the marriage was dissolved. The guilty wife was put away by her husband and turned out of her home or stoned.

Though the case in hand does not apply to a literal marriage, but to the covenantal relationship supposedly existing between Yahweh and Israel — a relationship even more intimate than that of marriage — it does presuppose a sense of mutual affection and devotion. Yahweh would be the nation's God if they would be His people. The evidence of their being His people would be their keeping the law (the words of the covenant). If, on the other hand, they forsook Yahweh, His first reaction would be to declare the dissolution of the relationship.

This first impulse on Yahweh's part can be seen in Hosea 2:3. Here, having fulfilled the responsibilities of a husband to clothe his wife (Exod. 21:10), he declared that he would strip her naked, a thing often done to unfaithful women. He would return her to the poverty which she knew when he found her in Egypt, "as in the day she was

26

born," that is, when she was without anything. Also, he would deny her fields their fertility — the very fertility which the people had been attributing to the Baalim. As a consequence, the population would perish — in this case from a famine brought upon the land, not by stoning, as in the case of the ordinary adulteress (see Deut. 22:22).

In addition to Yahweh's consideration of returning them to their premarital state, marked by infancy and poverty, He would have no mercy upon the offspring born to this unworthy union. Whether this was a reference to the actual progeny, or to the spiritual progeny, of the nation is open to question. In either case, the results would be the same. Yahweh felt like denying them His compassionate concern, and He seems to have entertained such a denial as His first consideration.

Now, add to these initial reactions another one, stated earlier in 2:3. There Yahweh considered taking back all which He had formerly given His bride (2:9). This idea gives some indication of what would have happened to Israel had Yahweh followed His initial impulse. He did not follow through with that, however. Ultimately, He chose a different course altogether.

3. *Yahweh's Ultimate Response to Israel's Shame* (2:6, 7a, 10, 11, 14, 15a). Though Yahweh's initial reaction is clearly outlined in the above section, He at last chose a different course. Instead of reducing Israel to poverty and want, He chose to convince her of the folly and futility of the way she had chosen. He would not seek her destruction. He would seek to persuade her to reject her present course in several ways.

The first method to be employed was to hedge her about with restraints. These were depicted as a hedge of thorns and a wall. Both would keep the nation from finding the "paths" which led to her aspirations (2:6). This was simply the prophet's way of saying that the rewards of her pursuit of the Baalim would be so disappointing they would serve as a deterrent (a hedge of thorns or a wall) which should convince her the desired results would never be realized in the direction she was going.

How different this response was to Yahweh's first reaction! Under these circumstances Yahweh did not seek Israel's destruction but her restoration. He wished her restored to her former role of wife. One way of persuading Israel to return to Yahweh was to convince her that the things she longed for would never be realized through the Baalim. To do this would require unusual restraints.

Much the same idea is reflected in the next verse (2:7a). Here Israel "follows after her lovers," but she will never "overtake them."

That is, she would never realize the things supposedly proffered by her false suitors; she would not "find them." The Baalim would never provide anything but one disappointment after another. That in itself was by providential design. Yahweh had ordained that Israel would never find satisfaction in the gods. Contentment could result only from their faithfulness to their covenant obligations.

After Yahweh's intervention, He set about to expose Israel as the shameful and loathsome creature she had become (2:10a). He would do this in spite of any assistance which might be expected from her paramours (2:10b). After all, they had never helped the nation in times past; so how could they be expected to come to her rescue now (2:10c)? As before, these gods would be no more than one disappointment after another. Yet, that disappointment would be used advantageously by Yahweh as He sought to turn Israel's affections back toward Himself and away from the Baalim.

In addition to convincing Israel of the inability of the Baalim to come to her rescue and after having revealed her shame, Yahweh considered cutting off the produce of the fields. In this way, He would deny the people food as well as resources required for their traditional festivals (2:11). Such a denial would have a salutary effect upon the inhabitants. It could encourage them to acknowledge the superiority of Yahweh over the Baalim. That in itself, as much as anything else, should have convinced them they had made a foolish choice.

All that we have considered thus far had the purpose of showing the superiority of Yahweh over Israel's lovers, the Baalim. Even so, Israel continually pursued these gods, but always to her disappointment. By now it had become crystal clear that Yahweh's role was different. Rather than being pursued by Israel, He was pursuing her. He longed to have Israel back; therefore, He refused to give her up. He would pursue her without ceasing. He would use every avenue, every means, to help her to see that He should be the object of her affection, and that she would never find the longings of her heart in another.

Yahweh's endless quest would involve His luring her into the wilderness — a wilderness created by the previously announced devastation — where there was nothing to distract her. There would be no Baalim there. There He would speak to her heart to heart (2:14). This generous action on Yahweh's part would open up the possibility of the restoration of the relationship which existed prior to the time of their forsaking Yahweh for the Baalim.

By now it must have been obvious that all Yahweh had been

considering, all He had anticipated doing by way of troubling Israel, and in His speaking comfortably to her, was for the purpose of providing an avenue of hope (2:15a). This avenue of hope, referred to as the valley of Achor (a symbol for troubling), was a reference to the place where Achan's disobedience to Yahweh was avenged (Josh. 7:26). It is a reference to the site where Yahweh's wrath was placated, a place which would provide an occasion for a renewal of their former relationship. That is, as the troubling over Achan became a door of hope for Israel in the past, the troubling caused by the worship of the Baalim would become a similar door of opportunity for Israel now. That, and the wooing of Israel by Yahweh, reflected in His continual quest for her, would open the way to renewed relations and to a future of happiness and success (2:15b). That way is to be considered in the following section.

4. *The Effects of Yahweh's Reaction and Response Upon Israel* (2:7b, 15b, 16-23). We may feel that Yahweh would have certainly been justified if He had followed His first reaction and destroyed Israel. Nevertheless, He chose rather to pursue her by means of disappointment, suffering and wooing. How different was His response from that of man! A man would have destroyed the nation for her unfaithfulness. Yahweh wanted to restore her. So He sought to win her back to Himself.

All that Yahweh did, in seeking the renewal of the relationship with Israel, had a profound effect upon the wife-nation. Because of her disappointment over the lack of benefits from the Baalim, Israel determined to return to her first husband, Yahweh (2:7b). She longed for things to be as they had been "then," that is, when Israel formerly followed Yahweh — during the wilderness journey — she saw that it was better for her then than now as she followed the Baalim. Thus, Yahweh's quest, through judgment and wooing, had a positive effect upon Israel. It, at last, resulted in her returning to her first Husband, Yahweh. She had seen the difference. She had benefited from her relationship with Yahweh while, in her relationship with the Baalim, she had experienced one disappointment and/or judgment after the other.

In addition to Israel's own declaration of her intention to return, Yahweh announced that the nation would respond positively. She would respond to the troubled conditions she had encountered by turning to Him with the same delight and willingness she had experienced when she followed Him out of Egypt (2:15b). This happy prospect could but result in her denial of any reference to Him as Baali, which was a legal reference to the husband as the master of his wife. She would return to her former lover whom she affectionately refers to as Ishi, a term of endearment meaning "my husband" and connoting the deep interpersonal relationship of marriage (2:16). The Baalim would, as a result, not only be eliminated from the nation's vocabulary; they would be forgotten altogether (2:17).

The happy prospects of the events just described, referred to in time as "in that day," would result in Israel's world becoming a place of peace and tranquillity (2:18a). These were conditions to be realized no doubt in the messianic age. It would be a time of peace among men, in part at least, resulting from the destruction of the implements of war (2:18b). At that time, Yahweh would, having by then transformed Israel, betroth her to Himself as His bride forever (2:19).

Out of that new and permanent betrothal (which may be a reference to the new covenant of Jeremiah — 31:31-34) would come a bride who would know Yahweh intimately, as well as one who would remain faithful to Him (2:20). Such intimacy and faithfulness would result, in turn, in Yahweh's goodness and faithfulness (2:21), and the nation's being permanently planted upon the land (2:23a). When that time finally came, those who had been unpitied would then be the objects of His pity, and those who had been referred to as not being His would be declared to be His very own people (2:23b). What a day that would be!

Thus, in this section, the Book of Hosea proclaims the truth that the overwhelming desire of Yahweh is not for the destruction of those who reject or turn from Him, but for their redemption and restoration, and to enhance these possibilities, Yahweh had embarked upon an endless quest to win them to Himself. His providences in such quests often result in men and nations turning to Him and their becoming the recipients of the most intimate of relationships, the beneficiaries of unbelievable provisions for life.

How wonderful to know that the One who sought Israel still seeks man through the spirit of His Son! How meaningful the truth that He still responds to those who respond to Him! It was good news in Hosea's day; it is good news in our day.

FOR FURTHER STUDY

1. Read the article on "Marriage" in IDB, Volume III, pp. 278-286 and in ZPBD, pp. 511-513.
2. Read the article on "Baal" in ZPBD, pp. 87-88, and in IDB, Volume I, pp. 328-329.

3. Discuss the grace of God reflected in chapter 2 of the Book of Hosea.
4. Does the New Testament place the same emphasis upon the material benefits of a proper relationship to God that are to be found in the Old Testament? If so, explain. If not, why not?
5. Do you believe God still has a first and second response as He deals with the sins of men and nations? Discuss.
6. How did Yahweh convince Israel of the folly of following the Baalim?
7. Does God still trouble men to get them to forsake other gods?

CHAPTER 4

A LOVE THAT TRANSCENDS
(Hosea 3:1-5)

1. Yahweh's Command to Love Again (3:1)
2. Hosea's Obedient Response to Yahweh's Command (3:2-3)
3. The Lesson for Israel (3:4-5)

Chapter 3 of Hosea has presented problems for some scholars, one of the first being a distinct difference between verses 1-3 and verses 4-5. It is suggested that the emphasis of verses 1-3 is upon the symbolic action of the prophet, while verses 4-5 are concerned with the future of the nation. While it must be acknowledged that a difference between the sections does exist, there seems to be little formidable evidence against the unity of the passage. In fact, the preponderance of evidence would appear to favor such a unity. The primary contention is that the response of the prophet toward Gomer is symbolic of Yahweh's attitude and response toward Israel. Such an approach greatly simplifies the whole matter and does provide a reasonable interpretation of the passage.

A second problem to be considered in one's approach to chapter 3 is whether it should remain in its present position or be made a continuation of chapter 2.

Those contending it is a continuation of 1:9 do so in the belief that these verses are the natural continuation of the account of Gomer's ultimate abandonment of her home and family in quest of the pleasures to be gained as a temple prostitute. Continuing in the same vein, these scholars suggest that in due course Gomer, after being used up as a prostitute, was offered for sale in the slave market. Finding her there the prophet was instructed to buy her back, which he did.

This may well be the most reasonable explanation of the events which transpired. If so, then it is reasonable to insist that chapter 3 is best understood as a continuation to chapter 2, because of its position in the book; that is, the theme of chapter 2 is continued in chapter 3.

Whether either of these explanations is a reasonable assumption or not, there is little ground for questioning whether the section is from Hosea. Though some argue the material is much later, or it is an allegory based on events in Hosea's experience, these are assumptions which cannot be proved. In addition, there are some who contend that Hosea, a northerner, would not look with favor on the reunion of the two nations to be ruled over by a prince from David's line. Such an argument is too subjective, and it ought to be kept in mind that Israel's golden age had always been associated with the age of David. It is, therefore, reasonable to believe that Hosea felt positively rather than negatively toward the restoration of David's line. It may, in fact, be the more reasonable supposition.

With this brief treatment of some of the problems suggested by this section, let us turn to a discussion of the content of the chapter.

1. *Yahweh's Command to Love Again* (3:1). Chapter 3 opens with a command to Hosea to "love again" one (Gomer, no doubt) who had been unfaithful to him, one who had sinned against him. It is noteworthy that the prophet was "commanded" to love. This is strange to modern man, who looks upon love as something to "fall" into, engage in sexually, or to carry out in a contract of marriage. For the prophet, however, there was nothing unusual about it. For him, love was a beneficent act, in response to the will of God, for another (cf. 11:1). It, like the love of Yahweh, defied justification or explanation. It was an active, tender, nonjudgmental response, placing whatever one had to offer at the disposal of another. It was the sharing of compassion and mercy when circumstances seemed to be pressing for the rejection of both. It was a warmth of feeling which found its ultimate expression in the Old Testament in Yahweh's attitude and action toward Israel, and in the New Testament in the giving of His Son — His best gift — for those who could not help themselves. Since it was so, it could be, and was, commanded: first of man to himself and then of man to his neighbor.

In the case at hand, Hosea was commanded to love "again a woman beloved of her friend, and an adulteress . . ." Though some object to identifying the woman as Gomer, contending it was not the prophet's wife, there is little to support such a position since the command involved loving *"again."* Having loved Gomer at the start, how could the prophet be commanded to love any other than Gomer again? How could it have been analogous to Yahweh's love for Israel, who had been as unfaithful to Him as Gomer had been to Hosea, if it had not been she?

Hosea was commanded to love Gomer as Yahweh loved Israel. That is, upon learning of Yahweh's attitude and response toward

33

Israel, Hosea was to display a similar attitude and respond in a like manner.

Yahweh's love for Israel had no basis for being as far as the nation was concerned. She (Israel) was, in fact, in love with "other gods," and the things (i.e., such things as blocks of raisins used in cultic feasts) used in her worship of them. In fact, the attitude and practices of Israel were such as would stifle Yahweh's love. Even so, His love was a spontaneous and beneficent response to the people's deepest need. Transcending every justification for withholding it, it reached out to embrace them, no matter their conditions. It did so because it was divine love.

Since Yahweh's love was one that transcended every basis of denial, Hosea's was to be the same kind. Therefore God commanded him to love Gomer, even though she had become an adulteress. If God could love Israel, after having been rejected by her, Hosea could love Gomer after having been forsaken by her.

2. Hosea's Obedient Response to Yahweh's Command (3:2, 3). Having been instructed in the nature of divine love, and having been commanded to love again the one who had betrayed his love, the prophet responded positively to Yahweh's command. He bought Gomer for fifteen shekels of silver (approximately nine dollars) and an homer and half (perhaps fifteen or sixteen bushels) of barley (3:2).

The claim that he bought her implies she was not her own woman, but was a slave. She had either sold herself into slavery, had been sold into slavery after fulfilling her role as a temple prostitute, or had been sold by one of her paramours. In any case, the effect was the same. She must now be bought for a price. Whatever the real situation, Hosea's response suggests a readiness and willingness on his part to do everything necessary — to pay any price, to overcome any obstacle — to reestablish the former relationship.

The ultimate reestablishment of the former relationship, however, was not to be immediate, as may first appear to be the case. The hurt had been too deep. Though in love with Gomer — perhaps all the while — he probably wanted sufficient time to elapse to encourage the return of her affection and loyalty to him. Therefore, he shut her away from all who might tempt her (3:3), while he himself refused to rush the resumption of their relationship. Time would be allowed for the dissipation of old infatuations and the rekindling of dissipated or dormant love. In due time normal relations would be resumed, but with caution and after assurance.

This experience of Hosea, actual and unusual in the human realm, to be sure, was nevertheless a miniature or parable of the larger experience which Yahweh had with the nation. Hosea's response was an indication of the way Yahweh would respond toward wayward Israel. To that experience we now turn.

3. *The Lesson for Israel* (3:4-5). That the experience of Hosea and Gomer reflected in verse 3 has implications beyond itself no one would question. In fact, it is generally agreed that what was done in the case of the prophet and his wife has a more extensive application than that relating to their own situation. It was a reflection of what Israel herself would be compelled to endure.

Israel would be cut off from king, prince, cult, and ritual, elements required for their national existence (3:4). Their separation from these essentials would be accomplished in the exile, and the exile would result from their forsaking Yahweh for other gods, much as Gomer had forsaken Hosea for other lovers. That separation from their land, and all which made it meaningful, would serve in its own way the same purpose as Hosea's act in shutting off Gomer. It would provide a context, and a time, in which Israel could reevaluate its former condition. It would also allow sufficient time for the restoration of former attitudes and feelings.

Following the exile, and after the nation had learned the price which its profligacy had cost, the people would "return, and seek Yahweh their God." In doing so, they would turn from their idolatrous practices (3:5a). Their allegiance would no longer be divided. The nation would give undivided allegiance to Yahweh and His purpose as reflected in the line of David (3:5b). In that restored relationship they would fear (reverence properly) Yahweh and become the beneficiaries of His goodness in "the latter days" (3:5c), that is, in the days generally associated with the messianic age.

Over and over throughout the prophetic books of the Old Testament, this emphasis upon the latter days is made. These days were days of anticipation when all the suffering, punishment, and denials of the past would be ended. There would be a return to the golden age of David. The nation would once more be strong and wealthy. All her enemies would be conquered, and relations with Yahweh would be what they should be. This time, so frequently referred to as "the latter days," was used as a reference to the messianic age — that ideal time would be established at some future date when the throne of David would be reoccupied and all of the potential of Israel would be realized.

FOR FURTHER STUDY

1. Do you believe the woman in chapter 3 to be Gomer? If so, does it present a problem that Hosea was commanded to marry one who had stooped so low? How do you deal with this problem? Discuss.
2. Does genuine love always respond spontaneously to human need? Is anything less a genuine expression? Discuss. What do you mean when you use the term love? How has it been misused and abused?
3. How does the command of God to love relate to our own day? Does it speak to the present situation? If yes, how? If no, why not? Discuss.
4. If it was possible for love which had been rejected to be rekindled in Hosea's day, is it not possible for it to be done in the modern world? Is it? If not, why not? If so, how? Discuss.
5. Read the article on "Exile" in ZPBD, pp. 265-267 and in IDB, Volume II, pp. 186-188.
6. Read the articles on "Messiah" in ZPBD, pp. 528-529, and on "Messiah, Jewish" in IDB, Volume III, pp. 360-365.

CHAPTER 5

WHEN RESPONSIBLE MEN FAIL
(Hosea 4:1-19)

1. Yahweh's Lawsuit Resulting From Israel's Moral Decline (4:1-2)
2. The Indictment of Israel's Leadership (4:4-8)
3. Yahweh's Sentencing of Israel and Her Leaders (4:3, 9, 10)
4. The Effect of Faltering Leadership Upon Religion (4:11-15)
5. A Stubborn Spirit and the Wind of Destruction (4:16-19)

Nothing is quite as revealing about a society, nor nearly so determinative, as the character of its leadership. Israel, though an elect nation, was no exception. The men in responsible positions in the nation — and at this point Hosea was primarily concerned with the religious leadership — had failed to provide the caliber of leadership necessary to assure the national well-being. That failure contributed to the nation's religious and moral decline and, ultimately, to their indictment and sentencing by Yahweh.

1. *Yahweh's Lawsuit Resulting From Israel's Moral Decline* (4:1-2). In the idiom of the lawsuit, chapter 4 opens with Hosea's summoning the nation to listen to the charges being brought against it. These charges, though communicated through the prophet, originated with Yahweh Himself, who served the dual role of being both prosecuting attorney and judge.

The offenses, which caused the charges to be brought in the first place, are stated both negatively and positively (4:1-2). The first negative charge brought was to the effect that there was no ground for mutual trust and confidence. This was caused by the disappearance of "truth" from the land. Society was full of distrust and suspicion. There was a lack of integrity on the part of the inhabitants. Men would speak, but their words were not trustworthy. They would act, but their transactions were not only ulterior, they were devious. This provided the prosecution with a formidable point, since society could not then, any more than it could now, survive the loss of truth.

The second negative charge was that there was no "goodness" in

37

Israel. The "goodness" (good will or warmth of feeling) which should have permeated the covenant society of Israel was lacking. One reason for this was the dissipation of truth, already referred to in the previous charge.

A more fundamental reason for the lack of goodness, however, is reflected in the third negative charge. It was the lack of a "knowledge of God." This charge had to do with their knowledge of His will and purpose for the individual as well as the nation — a will and purpose revealed through the law and the preaching of the prophets. The knowledge referred to involved more than an academic acquaintance with the law, however. It included a vital, transforming experience with Yahweh. As long as such an experience was lacking there could be no "truth" or "goodness" in the life and activity of Israel. Nor can there be in any other society, be it ancient or modern, because no society can possess "truth" and "goodness" in the final analysis without a profound "knowledge of God."

The second group of offenses with which Israel was charged was stated positively. These had to do with the breaking of the sixth, seventh, eighth, and ninth of the Ten Commandments. Interestingly enough, the order of their occurrence in Hosea is different from their order in the Decalogue in Exodus 20 and Deuteronomy 5. The reason for this is not clear. It may have been for the purpose of indicating the order of their frequency, that is, from the greatest frequency to the least. On the other hand, the order in Hosea may have been for the purpose of showing, in descending order, their danger for the community or for the provocation of the wrath of Yahweh. In any case, the breaking of the commandments reflected the people's attitude toward their covenantal responsibility.

It will be remembered that the second group of laws in the Decalogue has to do with a man's covenantal responsibility toward his fellow man. Israel was commanded to respect the rights of the individual to his life, his home, his possessions, and his character. But according to the prosecution, Israel refused to respect these rights (4:2).

The first charge, positively stated, was "swearing." This transgression probably took the form of a curse, an imprecatory prayer, or a man's calling upon Yahweh to witness a falsehood. It had the effect of denying one his right to truth. It may have even been an expression which reflected a contempt for human personality. Either or both of these made brotherhood an impossible dream and indicated how far the nation had digressed from the goal of mutual respect and appreciation which had been established for them by the covenant.

The second charge by the prosecution, from the positive side, was "lying" or "breaking faith." This condition, a common one in ancient Israel and in most societies, took the form of dishonesty and deception. It denied a man his right to fairness and justice in the market place and/or in a court of law. This taught that, as there could be no community without truth, there could be no society without justice.

The third charge was "killing." Though the Old Testament allowed for divinely authorized killing, it denied a man the right to slay a fellow being out of jealousy, hatred, or lust. Even so, Israel was charged by the prophet with unauthorized killings. This not only reflected a negative attitude toward their covenantal responsibility, it manifested a lack of respect for human life and personality.

The next thing with which they were charged was "stealing." Stealing denied a man's right to the material possessions entrusted to him by Yahweh, the ultimate owner of everything from the Old Testament standpoint.

Following the indictment for "stealing," the inhabitants of the covenant community were charged with "committing adultery." This was the transgression that denied a person his right to the integrity of his home. If the individual or family lacked virtue, the basic unit of society would be endangered. To jeopardize honor, mutual trust, or integrity as it related to the family could but raise a serious question about the future, and rightly so, because it is here that most civilizations, including that of ancient Israel, have been lost.

In 2:2b, the immediate effect of these transgressions is recorded. They were resulting in such widespread acts of violence, that one such deed "toucheth" another. That is, one murderous deed followed so soon after another that they are described as being connected to each other like links in a chain.

Thus, one charge after another had been brought against Israel (4:1-2). It was a sad state to which they had come. The moral decline within the nation had become so widespread that the controversy was referred to as being "with the inhabitants of the land." Even so, the primary blame was placed upon the leaders of the nation, as will become more obvious in the following section.

2. *The Indictment of Israel's Leadership* (4:4-8). While the entire population was charged with transgression in the preceding section, the prophet did not leave the matter there. He fixed the blame more definitely. He placed it upon the leadership, mostly upon the religious leadership.

Verse 4 opens with the suggestion that no one should bring a complaint, or words of reproof, against the population in general. The real complaint should be brought against the leaders. They were the most culpable of all. Because of the kind of leadership they were providing, they were condemned to perish ("stumble") in the light of day, when one would least expect such a happening (4:5a). That is, as one would not expect a person to trip over an obvious obstacle as he walked in the light of day, one would not expect the religious leaders, who should have known better, to be punished for failure to measure up to the highest standard of conduct. The priests, of all men, would be expected to escape the displeasure of Yahweh; not so with the priests of Israel, however. Neither was it so with the prophets. The revelation which they received in their dreams would become occasions for stumbling rather than examples to follow.

Not only would priest and prophet stumble because of their failure to provide proper leadership, there was the most unusual reference to "thy mother" (4:5c). This designation has been variously explained. One attempt suggests that it was a reference to the priesthood in general who would be punished along with their offspring (cf. Jer. 22:26; 1 Sam. 15:33). A second possibility is that it was simply a reference to the nation. Another possibility is that it was a reference to the family of some particular priest.

Whether any of these is the correct interpretation or not, a common theme is reflected through all of them. It is that the priests, as well as those who had been intimately associated with them, would suffer a similar punishment.

The knowledge which the nation lacked was a knowledge which should have been taught them by the priests. Their failure to teach, assessed as their having rejected knowledge and having forgotten the law, placed the responsibility for the destruction of Israel in large part upon their shoulders (4:6). Since the priests were so responsible for Israel's sin, judgment would not only come from Israel, but the priests would be rejected and their children forgotten. Their rejection would mean they would be excluded from their priestly function. And the forgetting would refer to Yahweh's ignoring those (their children) who would have inherited the office in years to come.

The tragic failure of the priesthood is further emphasized in 4:7, 8. In verse 7, the priests were accused of becoming more wicked as they grew in number, in possessions, and, no doubt, in power or influence. Instead of taking action to deter abusive power, materialism, and greed, the priests were encouraging them by their examples (4:7a). In doing so they had forfeited their honored position ("glory") and would be given one without honor instead (4:7b).

Verse 8 is an elaboration of the role chosen by the priests. Rather than being grief-stricken over the sins of the people, they delighted in, even cherished, the iniquitous acts of Israel; for the more the people sinned, the more numerous became the sacrifices. The more numerous the sacrifices, the more abundant became the resources of the priest (4:8) because they were the recipients of a portion of each sacrifice offered to Yahweh (1 Sam. 2:13-17). Therefore, the more the people sinned and sacrificed, the more the priests received, and the less interest they (the priests) had in dissuading the nation from sin. Thus, it is quite obvious that the leaders, as much if not more than the followers, had acted contrary to Yahweh's purpose for them and had led the people astray. Therefore, His displeasure.

3. *Yahweh's Sentencing of Israel and Her Leaders* (4:3, 9, 10). As a consequence of the iniquity of Israel, ultimately blamed upon their religious leaders, the land would be sentenced by the judge (Yahweh) of the divine court. This sentencing would be in the form of a drought so severe that the waters, not only those in the rivers but those in the seas as well, would vanish (4:3). The priests, who, presumably, might have been spared because of the quality of life which they should have been living as a result of their nearness to Yahweh, would suffer along with the rest of the population (4:9), because, if anything, they were worse. In their failure to lead, they had encouraged the nation to continue and even increase its sinning. As a result, they, too, would be denied the vast quantities of food required to meet their extravagant standard of living (4:10a). In addition, they would be rendered childless ("shall not increase") (4:10b); they would be left without successors.

4. *The Effect of Faltering Leadership Upon Religion* (4:11-15). Though, in an ultimate sense, a distinction between the effect of a faltering leadership upon morality and the effect upon religion may not be properly made, these aspects are discussed in separate places in chapter 4. The moral effect is discussed in verses 1 and 2, while the religious effect is considered in verses 11-15.

The latter section begins with a wisdom saying (4:11) which was probably in wide circulation at the time. Some suggest that the original subject of the saying was "new wine." It is presumed, therefore, that this was not a reference to drunkenness as such, but to the passionate longing of the people for the fruit of the vine in anticipation of its intoxicating effect. However, there is nothing against the possibility that both the fermented wine and the newly pressed juice were included in the saying. If so, the saying may have been descriptive of a common practice in Israel. As a result of their passionate longing for a continued abundance of wine (old and new), they would be driven to an idolatry (whoredoms) which would theoretically guarantee them wine in continued abundance. In that case the idolatry would be the old practice of the worship of the Baalim. The inhabitants, to assure their drink, turned to the worship of Canaanite deities who would, they falsely believed, guarantee the fertility that would provide them, continually and increasingly, with the fruit of the vine.

Verses 12 and 13 describe the ways the nation went about the worship of these Canaanitish deities. They, in part, sought direction from the wooden images (the Asherah). They, also, looked to "their staff," a possible reference to the Urim and Thummim, a diminuitive Asherah, or to the use of sticks or the casting of arrows (Ezek. 21:21) as a means of determining the direction one should take. In any case, these actions resulted from the overwhelming influence of idolatry upon the nation. That influence was referred to as "the spirit of whoredom." It was an influence which contributed to their rejection of Yahweh and to their submission to the gods of Canaan, which led them into one erring way after another (4:12*b*).

Their erring ways are stated in verse 13. They included the making of sacrifices at the high places ("tops of the mountains") which had been used as worship centers by the Canaanites. These were oases protected from the intense heat of the sun by the shade ("shadow") of the oak, the poplar, and the elm. The sacrifices were augmented by, or at least had as part of their ritual, sexual immoralities involving both single and married women (4:13*b*).

In addition to the profligacy of the women, as tragic as that was, the men were singled out for special condemnation because of their involvement in such sordid practices (4:14). This condemnation implied that the man had been behind the degrading activity from the first, and that Israel could not survive a double standard. Since the men were primarily responsible, the women would receive a lighter penalty (4:14*a*). And those who did "not understand," that is, those who had not been taught by the priests, who had followed the example of the men, and who, consequently, did not know ("understand") Yahweh's will and purpose, would find they had embarked upon the road to destruction (4:14*b*). To have chosen this direction was but one indication of the stubbornness of the nation, which would be rewarded with a destructive response from Yahweh.

5. *A Stubborn Spirit and the Wind of Destruction* (4:16-19). For Israel to have gone after idols was sufficient proof to establish that they had refused to submit to the will of God. They acted like an

obstreperous heifer which refused to go in the direction its master led. Since they willed not to follow their master, He (Yahweh) would grant them their wish. He would permit them to wander at will. Their wandering, however, would take them into the open country, where there would be no limits or protective barriers. Instead of boundaries or barriers they would find themselves vulnerable to the wild beasts inhabiting those vast unprotected areas (4:16). In addition to the dangers of the open country, their shameful practices ("play the harlot continually") (4:18) would bring a destructive force equal to that of a violent storm (4:19).

The greatest tragedy of all resulting from the failure of Israel's leadership was, no doubt, that of the prophet's being instructed to cease to minister to Israel (Ephraim). Those unable to give up their idols deserved no less (4:17). After all, the prophet's words would only be wasted because they would fall upon deaf ears. There appeared to be little likelihood now, that Israel would heed the prophet's call. Therefore, he was instructed to leave them alone, to leave them to their own choices.

One final point of consideration is found in verse 15. There Judah was advised not to become involved in idolatry as Israel had. The people of Judah were to be wiser than Israel and not equate the worship of Yahweh with the high places at Beth-aven or with those at Gilgal. To do so would provoke His displeasure and would cause them to be consigned to annihilation.

How tragic that a nation so providentially cared for should have everything brought into jeopardy because it followed unworthy leaders. But that is precisely what happened in the life of Israel. It was not the last time it has happened.

FOR FURTHER STUDY

1. Read the article on "Law in the Old Testament" in IDB, Volume III, pp. 77-89 and on "Law" in ZPBD, pp. 477-480.
2. Read the articles on "Truth" in IDB, Volume IV, pp. 713-717 and in ZPBD, pp. 872-873.
3. Read the article on the "Ten Commandments" in IDB, pp. 569-572.
4. What relationship did Hosea see existing between the leadership of the day and the conditions of his time? How did he handle this matter? Can we learn anything from the prophet in dealing with our own problems? Discuss.
5. Does God still punish societies in material ways? Have you wit-

nessed what you believe to have been such an action on His part? Discuss.

6. Does your society seem to have a double standard relating to the conduct of men and women? If so, how are these reflected? How should they be dealt with?

7. Is there a relationship between the success and failure of a prophet or minister and the attitude of the people he serves? If so, clarify and elaborate upon the matter. What can be done to resolve the problem?

CHAPTER 6

SIN, SHALLOW REPENTANCE AND GOD'S CONSTERNATION
(Hosea 5-6)

1. The Sinful Conditions Prevailing in Israel (5:1, 2, 10; 5:4, 7, 11*b*, 13)
2. Yahweh's Knowledge of and Attitude Toward Conditions in Israel (5:3, 5, 6, 8, 9)
3. Israel's Response to the Attitude and Knowledge of Yahweh (6:1-3)
4. Yahweh's Dismay Over Israel's Attitude and Action (6:4-11)

Having called the leadership to account in chapter 4, Hosea continued to press the point of their failure in chapter 5, and expanded his considerations in such a way as to include the entire nation. In addition, as in the preceding section, he discussed their effect upon Yahweh. Afterwards, he turned to consider Israel's reaction to Yahweh's attitude and Yahweh's costernation over her shallow response.

1. *The Sinful Conditions Prevailing in Israel* (5:1-2, 10; 5:4, 7, 11*b*, 13). Chapter 5 opens with a threefold command calling the hearers to give undivided attention to the sober words to follow. First, the priests were called upon to "hear this" (5:2*a*). Next, the "house of Israel" was commanded to give attention ("hearken") to the announcement which would follow. Whether the call to the "house of Israel" was a reference to the nation as a whole or not has been questioned. It has been suggested by some that such a general reference, between the commands to the priests and the court, leaves one with a problem. Yet, others have suggested that it may have been no more than an abbreviated reference to the clan leaders or to the elders of Israel. If so, the supposed problem created by a general reference appearing between two specific references would be resolved.

The third command ("give ear") was directed to the court. The court, as well as the priests and the house of Israel, was told that the judgment had been set (5:1*b*).

45

The reasons for the judgment were the sinful conditions found in every area of Israel's life. The leaders ("priests," "clan leaders or elders"), and the court ("house of the king") had contributed to those conditions through their failure to live up to their responsibilities. Rather than pointing those they led to freedom and a proper quality of life, the leaders had caused them to become ensnared by the cultic activities carried on at such places as Mizpah and Tabor (5:1*b*). Therefore, rather than being spiritual shepherds, they were characterized as hunters leading the people into one spiritual trap after the other. In addition, they were accused of having added depth to the pit. That is, they had dug the pit deeper. This was probably a reference to the activity at Shittim (5:2*a*). Shittim was always associated with the tragedy of Baal-peor (Num. 25:1ff.) in the memory of Israel. It had, no doubt, continued to exist through the years as a place of idolatry and immorality, or, as the marginal reference suggests, "in corruption."

In addition to the charges made above, the princes were accused of being "like them that remove the landmark" (5:10*a*). To have been accused of such an act could point in any number of directions. It could be interpreted to mean that they were instrumental in the removal of all bounds, the elimination of all personal restraints in the life of the nation. That is, there would be no acknowledgment of private rights at all. What was one person's possession, or presumed right, could be that of another if he wished to usurp it. On the other hand, this may have been a reference to the changing of the boundary line between Israel and Judah after the threat of the coalition of Syria and Ephraim, or it may have even been a reference to the changing of Judah's boundary by Asa some years earlier (1 Kings 15:22). On the other hand, a more viable option is that it was no more or less than a simple reference to the injustices of the time reflected in deceptive and oppressive designs which were perpetrated in order that some people might lay hold of the property of others. All rights were ignored. Traditional practices as well as Mosaic law were flouted, and this accumulation of evil could but provoke Yahweh to wrath (5:10*b*).

After having described the conditions resulting from the failure of Israel's leaders, Hosea focused attention upon the nation in general. Its condition was characterized as beyond the possibility of a change for the better (5:4*a*). The people had been so influenced by their leaders ("the spirit of whoredom in their midst"), and so committed to the idolatry which they encouraged, that they had reached a point of no return. Worse still, they did not know Yahweh (5:4*c*). That is, they (the nation) no longer knew Him in an intimate or redemptive way. The relationship which had existed between them no longer existed. The nation had turned to the gods of Canaan. The people had forsaken the fountain of life for cisterns which could hold no water (see Jer. 2:1ff.). Hosea described this action as "treacherous" (5:7a). The word for "treachery" means to be "faithless" or "deceitful." It was most frequently used with reference to faithlessness and deceit in the most intimate of relationships (marriages, covenants, etc.).

As a consequence of Israel's faithlessness, "they have borne strange children." That is, they had either borne children conceived while they were engaging in the cultic practices of Canaan, or they had produced a generation, following their fathers' example, to whom Yahweh was not known (5:7b).

Meanwhile, unable to leave the issue of a failing leadership, Hosea charged that Israel had been subjected to judgment (the Assyrian invasion?) because they had been content to follow the command of man (5:11). That is, they had been all too willing to follow the direction set by their leaders, and that direction may have been first set under the questionable advice given by Jeroboam I at the time of the founding of the new kingdom of Israel (see 1 Kings 12:28-33). If so, the prophet was placing the greater blame for Israel's folly, as well as the subsequent judgment, upon the advice of the leader(s). Even so, they were not the only ones responsible. The nation itself must bear her part of the responsibility for being so willing to follow her leaders. The people had suffered as a result of their folly, and they would suffer still more (5:12). Yet, when the citizens of Israel saw the ominousness of their condition, the miserable state resulting from Yahweh's judgment — the instrument chosen — they would acknowledge their wound ("sickness") as grievous. But, instead of turning to Yahweh in repentance, they would turn to their neighbor (Assyria). In doing so they would but learn that the Assyrians could not "heal" them. Their real enemy was not a political one. The real opponent was Yahweh, and Assyria would never be able to subdue or dissuade Him (5:13b).

In this remarkably logical and forceful way, Hosea had dealt with the sinful conditions in Israel. He first considered the contribution of the leaders to the prevailing conditions. Then he turned his attention upon the general conditions reflected in the nation as a whole. The nation had followed its leaders faithfully; but the path had led away from God rather than to Him, and this had profoundly altered His attitude toward the entire population.

2. *Yahweh's Knowledge of and His Attitude Toward Conditions*

in Israel (5:3, 6, 8-9, 11*a*-13, 15). The conditions within Israel were not concealed from Yahweh. He was fully cognizant of their idolatry and its resultant defilement (5:3). Their attitude toward what they were doing was one of contentment — yea, pride (5:5*a*). They took satisfaction in their devotion to ritual without any consideration of the necessity of turning to God in genuine repentance. For this failure they should expect nothing but destruction. The disaster would not only overtake Israel, however, it would befall Judah as well, because she had grown as wicked as Israel (5:5*a*).

The destruction was already on its way. It was just a matter of time now. The warning signaling the approach of the enemy needed to be sounded (5:8). Ritual would not save them now. Their festivals ("new moons") — their perfunctory ritual — would, on the other hand, provoke widespread disaster (5:7*b*); and Ephraim would become a desolation (5:9). The nation would be devastated by an oppressive enemy who would march through the land (5:11*a*), and by Yahweh's own unheralded and unnoticed intervention, which the prophet compared to the unseen work of the moth and the silent devastation of decay (5:12).

In verse 14 the extent of the judgment of Yahweh is compared to the fierceness of the lion falling upon its victim, tearing flesh from bones, and bearing the remains to its lair, from whence no other animal would attempt to retrieve the mutilated carcass (5:14). Both Ephraim and Judah were as helpless as the victim of the lion. They could no more expect to be retrieved from the clutches of an angry God — "there shall be none to deliver" — than one could expect the victim of the lion to be delivered.

In this way, Hosea had revealed Yahweh's total knowledge of Israel's sin (they believed they had concealed their sin behind a religious facade — 5:6). They had not succeeded, however. Their sin had been open and obvious to Yahweh all the while. It had provoked His judgment, a judgment so sure that no human devices could avert it. Though the nation would try desperately, by means of shallow repentance, it could never be realized that way.

3. *Israel's Response to the Attitude and Knowledge of Yahweh* (6:1-3). Having been warned of Yahweh's displeasure and the potential destruction resulting from it, Israel turned to ritual in the belief it would placate Yahweh's wrath and provide the means whereby they might ingratiate themselves to Him (5:5*a*). The first paragraph of chapter 6 (verses 1-3) indicates that genuine repentance was lacking. It is believed by some that these words were composed and put in the mouths of the people by Hosea. It seems more likely, however, that

they may have been words of the priests encouraging the nation to continue its traditional and meaningless ritual. Whether this be so or not, the point of the passage is the same. The words of repentance place the emphasis upon the people's wounds and their desire to be healed when the emphasis should have been upon their sin. This may be clearly seen in verse 1. The call to return to Yahweh came because He had torn and smitten. It did not reach to the real problem, sin, which could not be cared for in the healing and binding up. It could only be cared for through genuine repentance.

In addition to believing that their turning to God (though their repentance was not genuine) would bring healing, the people believed the healing would come in a relatively short time (6:2). Though the number of the days, as used here, implies an indefinite period of time, the reference to so few days does suggest an anticipated early response. They believed that Yahweh would speedily restore them to their former state (cf. Ezek. 37:1-10), after which they would presumably live "before him." That is, they would continue living under His protective care.

Verse 3 contains an exhortation to "know" Yahweh. It was an attempt to correct the charge that they had been destroyed because they did *not* know Him in the intimate way that they should (cf. Hosea 4:6). They believed their quest to know Him would ultimately result in His beneficence being as extensive and significant for them as the rains were to the earth. If the reference to the rain(s) included both the former and the latter rains, then the point was upon their essential nature, because both were necessary if a crop was to be produced. When both came in their seasons, an abundant harvest was assured. If one or the other was lacking, the crop was affected. Therefore, the priests were presumably attempting to assure the nation of the abundant blessings of Yahweh which would result from their gaining a more intimate knowledge of Him and thus being in a proper relationship to Him.

As noble as were the exhortations and encouragements found in 6:1-3, an essential factor was missing. There was no clear word of repentance. Though they may have intended their actions to convey an attitude of repentance, they seem to have reflected no more than sorrow and regret because they suffered. There was no evidence of sorrow over sin. Their only concern was with being healed and bound up — restored to their former wholeness. They were not interested in being restored to a proper relationship with Yahweh.

That this seems to be the right interpretation of their response is seen in Yahweh's reaction to what they did. He reacted with dismay.

4. *Yahweh's Dismay Over Israel's Attitude and Action* (6:4-11). Israel's desire to be healed was provoked by the pain they suffered as a result of Yaweh's displeasure, not because of sorrow for wrongdoing. This was shallow repentance. It did not reach to the heart of the matter. It did not come to grips with their sin. Therefore, Yahweh reacted with dismay. He raised the question as to what else it would take to move the population of the nations in the direction of genuine repentance (6:4a).

It was quite obvious that something more than what had been done was necessary. The spirit required for genuine repentance, if manifested at all by the nations, was as temporary and as transitory as the early mist or the morning dew (6:4b). There was no permanence to it at all. Therefore, it was not genuine repentance, since a true spirit of repentance is an abiding aspect of human experience. It is a permanent part of one's experience. Anything less is not enough.

The shallow repentant spirit of both Israel and Judah had motivated Yahweh to send the prophets. Their purpose was that of molding ("heaving") the nations into the shape which Yahweh decreed they should acquire. This had been done in part by the prophets, and in part by Yahweh's judgments (6:5b). That is, the prophets had contributed to the shape of the nations, while Yahweh's words had brought terrifying judgments which had not only revealed ("as light") Yahweh's purpose, but had hopefully moved the people toward the realization of it.

Verse 6 elaborates upon Yahweh's will or purpose for His people. When considered in the context, the prophet was decrying the popular attitude that all one must do to be in good standing with Yahweh was to follow the Mosaic ritual. More was involved than that. Yahweh was demanding that along with ritual there must be a genuine spirit of repentance. He was pressing the point that true religion was more than form. It had finally to do with one's inner spirit and attitude. Ritual alone would never result in the inauguration of or the renewal of the divine-human relationship. There must be an intimate and vital relationship based upon a personal knowledge of Yahweh and His purpose. Thus the call for "goodness, and not sacrifice; and the knowledge of God more than burnt-offerings."

The remainder of chapter 6 contains a list of the misdeeds of Israel and a statement of judgment upon Judah.

The section begins with the charge that Israel had "transgressed the covenant" (6:7a). That is, they had broken some covenant, the breaking of which was said to be "like Adam." To have compared it with the activity of Adam has been variously explained. Some contend that it is definitely a reference to Adam's disobedience to the command of Yahweh in the beginning, because the relationship in Eden depended upon man's response to that command. Others believe it is a reference to an unidentified incident in the recent past, and at a place called Adam. It may, on the other hand, have been a reference to the covenant at Sinai. Though scholars have been unable to resolve the difficulty, the action denounced was the failure of Israel to act as a responsible covenant-keeping people. They had performed like ordinary men who had never accepted a covenantal responsibility and were, consequently, charged with treachery (6:7b).

One of those treacherous deeds had taken place at Gilead, a city some distance north and east of the Jabbok (6:8a). Gilead was guilty of some violent act which had resulted in much human bloodshed (6:8b). This may have even been a form of human sacrifice. Whatever the case it was an activity in which only treacherous men would engage.

Another activity condemned by the prophet at this time, was related to Shechem, one of the cities of refuge (Josh. 20:7) which had been established in ancient Israel (6:9). Of all places in which a man could find protection and security it was expected it would be at one of the refuge cities. This was not the case at Shechem, however. If anything, life was worse there than elsewhere. The very highways leading to the city were inhabited by "troops of robbers" preying on those fleeing for asylum. And among the robbers were, of all men, the priests. Thus, one may readily see the condition at Shechem, one referred to as the committing of "lewdness" (outrage). Such outrage could be seen in the fact that a poor man, fleeing for the safety of the properly designated city of refuge, could not even find security for himself there. The times were so evil, in fact, that even the religious leaders joined hands with the robbers to plunder and murder the helpless population.

Verses 10-11 serve as a kind of summary of the conditions existing in both Israel and Judah. The first reference is to Israel's activity, which is referred to as "a horrible thing." That is, their idolatry ("whoredom") had resulted in the shameful and abominable deeds described in the preceding verses. All of these together had defiled the land. They had committed "a horrible thing." Israel was not alone, however. Judah, too, was to suffer for her evil (6:11a). Her judgment ("a harvest") was to take the form of an exile — the most dreaded of all punishments.

Thus, in chapters 6-7, Hosea called attention to the sinful conditions he found in both of the nations. He dealt with their casual way of trying to come to grips with these conditions through shallow repentance. In addition, he revealed Yahweh's dismay over their approach to the resolution of their pathetic state. Yahweh would never accept their effort. It would require more than the shallow repentance expressed by them. Nothing less than a genuine spiritual experience with the covenant God would suffice. Until they arrived at such an experience they could expect nothing but one judgment after the other.

FOR FURTHER STUDY

1. Read the articles on "Shittim" found in IDB, Vol. IV, p. 339 and in ZPBD, p. 789.
2. Read the articles on "Baal-peor" in IDB, Vol. I, p. 332 and in ZPBD, p. 88.
3. Read the articles on "Landmark" found in IDB, Vol. III, p. 66 and in ZPBD, p. 475.
4. Do you see any lessons for our own society coming from the situation in Israel as reflected in Hosea 5 and 6? What are they? Have they been taken seriously by your generation? If so, how? If not, why not?
5. When do international agreements become wrong for a nation? Do we have agreements with nations which you feel to be questionable? Which one(s)? Why? Discuss.
6. Do you believe God still reacts toward nations as He did toward Israel? Is there still a corporate responsibility? Discuss.
7. Are there still those who believe religion involves ritual alone? Who are they? Why do they believe such? What role does ritual have in your own life? What is more important as you see it?

CHAPTER 7

LIKE A DECEITFUL BOW
(Hosea 7:1-16)

1. A Definition of Deceit (7:16*b*)
2. Some Evidences of Israel's Condition (7:1-8, 13*a*).
3. The Characterization of Those Who So Conduct Themselves (7:8*b*, 11, 16*b*)
4. The Results of Israel's Condition (7:2*b*, 7-9*b*, 12-13*b*)
5. God's Plan for Israel Thwarted (7:1, 13*b*, 16*b*)

Nations, as well as those individuals who have been the beneficiaries of Yahweh's special care, would be expected to remain faithful to their benefactor. Yet, it is obvious that such has not been the case.

Israel, above all other nations, had been the recipient of God's providential care. She had experienced His elective grace and His promise that she would ultimately triumph over all of those opposing her. For these reasons, if for no others, it would have been expected of her that she remain loyal and faithful to Yahweh. Yet, she failed to do so. She deceived and forsook the one to whom she owed her very existence (Compare Amos 9:7).

1. *A Definition of Deceit* (7:16*b*). In verse 16, Hosea accused Israel of being deceitful. A deceiver is one who misleads, deludes, or cheats. As used in the case of Israel, it characterized her as being as unreliable as a bow whose arrows fall short of the target or deviate from their course instead of moving toward it. Therefore, as the arrow, misdirected by the bow, did not reach its goal, Israel had been misdirected in such a way that she had failed to reach the goal fixed for her by Yahweh. Thus, a deceitful nation — and Israel was one — is a nation which does not accomplish the goal or purpose set for it by its founder. In Israel's case the founder was Yahweh, and this but compounded the tragedy because the nation reflected little that would cause one to expect Yahweh had brought her into existence. In fact, conditions within the nation would suggest just the opposite.

2. *Some Evidences of Israel's Condition* (7:1-8, 13*a*). Israel, like a

deceitful bow (7:16*b*), did not respond to the noble purpose which had been set for her. Rather than being a righteous nation, she had become a society filled with iniquity (deviousness) (7:1). Dishonesty was widespread. Truth had been replaced by falsehood (7:1b). Thieves were plundering ("entereth in") house after house in city after city. Robbers (highwaymen) gathered in bands to prey upon those traveling the highways (7:1b). It was an unbelievable state to which Israel had come.

The leaders had made their contribution to the state of things in Ephraim (Israel). In fact, the king, supposedly Yahweh's representative, and the one citizen who should have set a worthy example, not only failed to be such; he found delight in the widespread "wickedness" of the day (5:3*a*). He was not alone. The other members of the royal family ("princes"), or those in command of the military forces who may have been referred to as "princes" (5:3*b*), delighted in the same lack of righteousness.

All levels of society — the king, the princes, and the citizenry — were guilty of immorality. Their passions were as intense as the smoldering fire of an oven waiting to receive the raised dough. When the dough was finally baked, the process of refiring would have to be begun again. This cycle was used as an analogy of the nation's pursuit of the gratification of their passion. There was a time when the fire of lust would die down; but in due time it would turn back to its prior passionate state ("leavened" state). When that condition occurred, the fire was rekindled to bring their passion (the leavened dough) to fruition by "baking" (7:4).

These passions, which in Israel's less compromising days had been hidden from public view, were now openly practiced. For instance, on state occasions, the king joined in drinking until he and his royal party, consisting of those who scoffed at prudence and virtue, became ill from their excesses (7:5). By such conduct they brought disgrace upon themselves and upon the society which they governed.

Verses 6-7 continue the oven incident after what some believe to have been a parenthetic point of reference in verse 5. These verses state that the oven smolders during the night while the leaven works (passion rebuilds), and the baker sleeps (7:6*a*). Next morning, after the leaven has worked, the fire is rebuilt and the process is completed in the baking of the dough. In a comparable cycle, the passions of the king, the princes, and the populace were brought to their climax in one immoral practice after another — even to the unbelievable point of the assassination of some of their leaders (7:7*a*). It was an evil time (see 2 Kings 15) — a time when men seemed to have forgotten Yahweh altogether. No one looked to Him though He provided their only hope. They had taken things into their own hands, and they evidently liked it that way. But the more they took into their own hands, the less they left in Yahweh's and the more perilous their future.

3. *The Characterization of Those Who So Conduct Themselves* (7:8b, 11, 16b). In attempting to resolve their problems — particularly their political problems — the people neglected to turn to Yahweh. Instead, they turned to Assyria. By seeking help from Asyria, after the murder of Pekah (2 Kings 15:29), Israel not only found herself subjected to them; she now felt herself obligated to adopt their social and cultic customs (7:8a). This adoption of foreign practices placed Israel's future in grave danger. Her only hope was now as it had always been, Yahweh, but, as seen above (7:7b), she refused to call upon Him. Time was running out for the nation. Even so, Israel could not be turned. She remained committed to the ways of the Assyrians. She was like a cake which could have been turned, yea, should have been, but had not (7:8b). That is, Israel could have turned to Yahweh, and she should have, but she did not. She remained with her wrong choices until she was ruined (burned) as a cake which had not been turned as it was being cooked.

Had the people, on the other hand, sought Yahweh before permanent injury came, they would have been spared great suffering. They would not have missed their chance of being properly "cooked." Yet they remained on one side — the Assyrian or Egyptian side — and failed to turn (being turned) at the right time to Yahweh's side. Thus, they missed their opportunity. Israel was a cake not turned. The nation was half ruined already. She was in such a state because she had committed herself to the way of foreigners. She had wandered from Yahweh and had remained away from Him (7:13a). Israel was a cake unturned. She had missed her opportunity. She was overcooked on one side and uncooked on the other. In such a condition, she was useless.

After having been characterized as "a cake not turned," Israel was described as being "like a silly dove" (7:11). This was the prophet's way of saying that the nation's foreign policy reminded him of a dove flitting from one place to another in search of security and the necessities of life.

Israel, in fact, had no fixed policy. That is, the people did not fix their policy, as they should have, by looking to Yahweh and remaining set in their course. They turned to Assyria when threatened by

Egypt or some other nation, and they turned to Egypt when threatened by Assyria or the others. As a consequence, they never did find the resources or the security they sought. That was because Egypt and Assyria were in no position to provide either. Security could be found only in Israel's remaining true to Yahweh. This they were unwilling to do. Because of that, they were likened to a dove — a silly dove at that. And so they never ceased their flitting from one place to another.

A third characterization used by the prophet, and referred to earlier, was that Israel was "like a deceitful bow" (7:16*b*). That is, they were as unreliable as a bow which fails to eject its arrows with the kind of accuracy that assures their reaching the target set for them. Israel, "like a deceitful bow" could not be counted upon. She had failed to accomplish the goal set for her. That is, she either fell short of or deviated from the target set for her by the known (manifest) will of Yahweh. She could not be depended upon to do the right thing, to move the right way. She always insisted on doing the wrong thing or choosing the wrong way. This insistence had a telling effect upon the nation.

4. *The Results of Israel's Condition* (7:2*b*, 7-9*b*, 12-13*b*). The people of Israel were beset by sin on every hand. Sin had encircled ("beset them about") them. Enmeshed in their own wicked devices, they had constructed their own demise. That in itself was destructive enough, but that was not all that had happened. There was the dreadful realization that their sins were known to Yahweh, and that He would continue to remember what they had done (7:2*b*). That included the fact that their hearts burned not with fire like an oven, but with one devious plot after another (7:7). By intrigue they removed four of their kings, and at the same time toppled those lesser officials (princes?) who had been charged with the responsibility of seeing that right and justice prevailed in the land. This was a duty which was never taken too seriously by any of them, however.

All the while, Israel's sins were open and manifest before Yahweh and He held her responsible for her actions. As a result, a silent and unobservable decay had already begun destroying her. The nations to whom Israel had turned for help (7:8, 11) had, instead of strengthening her, caused the depletion of her strength (resources) without her even being aware of it (7:9*a*). They had brought the nation to old age, as was now reflected in the "gray hairs . . . here and there upon her" (7:9*b*). That is, time for the nation had about run out. Old age was catching up with her. Life was swiftly ebbing away. She had come upon her last days, and she was not even aware of it ("knoweth it not").

These tragic circumstances resulted from the people's having turned from the only true source of help, Yahweh, and their having wandered from nation to nation (7:13). As a consequence destruction was decreed for them — a destruction from which Yahweh had tried to "redeem them" but one from which they would not be turned.

5. *God's Plan for Israel Thwarted* (7:1, 13*b*, 16*b*). Throughout chapter 7, the prophet kept reminding Israel of the potential of a nobler way than the one which they had chosen. Yahweh had planned to redeem the nation. But the more He tried, the more deceptive they became. When He turned to them to heal them, He but uncovered more and worse sins (7:1). Meanwhile, to the wickedness of their society, they added the evil of false repentance. They had, though knowing of their need, dealt treacherously with the most determinative factor in human experience (7:13*b*). They had turned, but not to Yahweh (7:16*b*). Though the goal was obvious, they went in the wrong direction. They were "like a deceitful bow." They never did reach the goal Yahweh had for them. They missed it, and that miss finally cost Israel her existence and gave the Egyptians another occasion to hold her in derision (7:16*b*).

FOR FURTHER STUDY

1. Read the articles on "Providence" found in IDB, Vol. III, p. 940 and in ZPBD, pp. 692-693.
2. Read the articles on "Election" in IDB, Vol. II, pp. 76-82 and ZPBD, p. 242.
3. Read the article on "Sin, Sinners" found in IDB, Vol. IV, pp. 361-376 and the article on "Sin" in ZPBD, p. 796.
4. What were some evidences that Israel's repentance was not genuine? Do you see any parallels between the conditions in Israel and those in your own society?
5. Do you believe your nation is moving toward the goal which God has set for it? In what way? If not, why not? Discuss.
6. How would you describe the conditions in our world today? What hope do you see? Discuss.

CHAPTER 8

ISRAEL AND HER FORGOTTEN MAKER
(Hosea 8-10)

1. Israel's Forgetfulness of Who Yahweh Was and What He Had Done (8:1-2, 4, 11, 14; 10:1)
2. Israel's Casting Off All That Was Good (8:3-6, 13; 9:1, 7b-9, 10b-15; 10:2b-4, 9)
3. Israel Remade in the Image of Her Lovers (9:10, 13)
4. The Days of Visitation, the Days of Recompense (9:2-7a, 11, 16-17; 10:2b, 5-8, 10-11, 14-15).
5. Time to Seek Yahweh (10:12)

The tragic failure of Israel during Hosea's ministry could be blamed in large part upon the fact that the nation had forgotten who Yahweh was and what He had done for them. This failure had inaugurated a period of moral, ethical, and religious decline that deeply affected Israel's relationship with Yahweh, and which set them upon a path that could but result in disaster should they insist upon pursuing it. The material contained in this chapter will deal with the tragic results of a nation who forgets her Maker.

1. *Israel's Forgetfulness of Who Yahweh Was and What He Had Done* (8:1-2, 4, 11, 14; 10:1). The relationship between Yahweh and Israel was unique. It went back in one way to the call of Abraham, and in another to the Exodus event.

Years after the death of Abraham his seed had gone to Egypt to escape a famine and had remained there to become a slave people. It was in such a state that Yahweh found them. When He did, it was an experience which was as delightful to Him as that of a lonely and hungry desert traveler who unexpectedly comes upon an oasis whose vines are laden with delicious fruit, or as joyful as that of the orchard keeper upon discovering the first, and often the best, fruit of the season (9:10). Israel was discovered of all places, in Egypt. Yahweh found her, and it was to His delight. She was, as it were, a luxuriant vine (10:1). But ere long, delight gave way to disappointment. The nation soon forgot the One who had not only found her but had made her what she was (8:14).

Forgetting her "Maker" encouraged Israel to forget the covenant made at Sinai (8:1). The people's actions made it appear as if they
had never been party to the Sinai agreement. It was forgotten and
ignored. This fact became increasingly obvious as Israel contracted
with the nations and turned to idols which they made of gold and
silver (8:4).

They not only acted as though no covenant existed between
them and Yahweh, they treated the law which He gave her (a special
mark of divine favor) "as a strange thing" (8:12). It was as if the law did
not exist for them. The laws referred to may have been those of the
book of the covenant (Exod. 21-23) or of some other segment of the
Mosaic legislation. Whatever the case, the laws were being ignored,
forgotten, and violated by Israel. She continued to erect one altar
after another, but not for the purpose of honoring Yahweh. They
were for the purpose of sacrificing to other gods (8:11). They ignored
the law which forbade such practices. They forgot the One who called
them into being.

In these verses Hosea came to grips with the tragic consequences of Israel's forgetfulness. Having forgotten their Maker, they
had drifted farther and farther from Him and had moved closer and
closer to the pagan deities worshiped in their midst. By doing so,
Israel cast off all that was good and worthwhile.

2. *Israel's Casting Off All That Was Good* (8:3-6, 13; 9:1, 7b-9,
10b-15; 10:2b-4, 9). Having forgotten Yahweh her Maker, having
failed to continue as a fruitful vine, having broken the covenant and
treated the law as something strange, Israel was forced to find a new
commitment for herself. This new commitment could but involve her
with some other god, a different purpose, or a different set of laws. As
she chose a new direction, and Israel did just that, she jeopardized all
that Yahweh had purposed for her — all that was good (8:3a). She
substituted other gods for Yahweh, made other contracts to take the
place of the covenant, and put her faith in her own devices, as will be
seen in the subsequent discussion.

Though kingship was at first denied Israel, in due course the
monarchy was established, but only with Yahweh's approval (1 Sam.
8:4-22). He alone held the prerogative to designate the one who was
to become the sovereign. The office was under Yahweh's control.
Whatever else this may have implied, it suggested a great potential
for the monarchy. Yet, during her last years Israel had permitted one
usurper after another to ascend the throne. These would often acquire their positions by murdering their predecessors (see 2 Kings

15:23ff.) and any surviving claimants ("princes"). By doing so they had established a new kind of nobility (8:4). It was a harmful thing which was done, and as they did it, it became another occasion for casting off the good.

Still another case of Israel's casting off the good was her rejection of Yahweh for idols made of gold and silver (8:5b-6). One such idol was the calf at Samaria. No doubt, it represented all of the bulls erected in other cities. Yahweh, in righteous indignation and disappointment over the nation's inability to maintain her innocence by remaining dedicated to that which was good, committed Himself to the destruction of the calf (8:5).

In light of Israel's relationship to Yahweh, He found the idolatrous practices hard to believe. These man-made idols which were 'not gods' were the reasons for Yahweh's judgment and destruction (8:6). The places of worship ("altars"), presumably set up for the purpose of caring for sin, were in themselves occasions for sin (8:11). This was so because the primary motive for these sacrifices was not the restoration of a right relationship with Yahweh, it was an effort at satisfying their insatiable appetites (8:13a). These self-centered occasions would never meet the requirement of Yahweh. He would reject all such offerings. Instead of forgiving "their iniquity," He would recount their sins and bring a judgment upon them comparable to the bondage of Egypt (8:13b). That is, Israel would return to the unbearable conditions which they had experienced while in Egypt (by returning to Egypt).

In chapter 9, Hosea continued to deal with Israel's idolatry. The occasion for these words was a religious festival held for the apparent purpose of celebrating the time of ingathering. Hosea, however, saw through the presumptuousness of these occasions (9:1). It was plain to the prophet that despite all the bounty Yahweh had bestowed at the ingathering, Israel celebrated the feast like the heathen nations around them. They did not credit Yahweh with anything. They played the harlot, "departing from . . . God." That is, they followed the immoral cultic practices of idolators, as though the occasion to celebrate had come as a reward ("hire") for immorality (9:11).

All through these years, Israel remained adamant in the face of Hosea's warning. In fact, she turned upon him in contempt, accusing him of being a madman (9:7). This idea seems to continue into verse 8 — a verse fraught with difficulty — where, as some believe, the prophet was claiming the role of Ephraim's watchman, a role which placed him in constant danger because he was compelled to condemn the wicked nation. He saw himself threatened by "the fowler's snare." That is, he was treated like an animal being hounded with one trap after the other, even "in the house of his God." Such conduct on Israel's part reminded the prophet of the conditions which had existed "in the days of Gibeah" (see Judges 19:22-30; 10:46-48). Hosea saw himself and the other prophets treated as harshly by their own people as the Levite had been treated by the Benjamites of Gibeah. This being so, the nation would be punished just as Benjamin of old had been (9:9*b*).

It has become increasingly obvious that Israel, after having been found by Yahweh — and to His delight at that — had turned away from Him to worship other gods. One of these was the Baal of Peor. This was a god (Num. 25:3) which had been worshiped on Mount Peor (Num. 25:28). By doing so, the nation had consecrated herself to a thing of shame (a word often used as a substitute for Baal) (9:10*b*). She had, as on other occasions, cast off a good thing for that which profited nothing. In fact, these actions, comparable to those in Gilgal (Amos 4:4; 5:5), had not only profited them nothing, they had forced Yahweh to drive them from His presence ("drive them out of my house") (9:15).

That nation ("a luxuriant vine"), which should have brought forth good fruit in abundance, had turned away from Yahweh to build altars for one pagan god after the other. Here they made offerings to such as the Baalim who the people believed to be a source of their prosperity (10:1). All the while they were manifesting their divided allegiance (10:2) — a condition which was intolerable if they were to be the people of Yahweh. Now it becomes clear they had cast off the good by trying to belong to the Baalim at the same time they claimed Yahweh as their God. Such folly could but fail on both sides. The people did not really belong to either Yahweh or the Baalim. Theirs was a divided loyalty which was, in the end, disloyalty to both sides.

Evidently the judgment (verse 2), resulting from their having compromised themselves with the Baalim, forced from them a confession. They recognized that the king — a usurper, no doubt, who had been enthroned without consultation with Yahweh — could do nothing to relieve the nation (10:3). They were, in fact, at the mercy of their enemies. Their choices had led them, once again, to cast off the good and their having done so resulted in their being cast off by Yahweh.

Verse 4 contains the same emphasis as that stated above. In this case, the nation was making covenants with the Assyrians and/or Egyptians. By doing so, Israel was casting off one of the benefits of the Sinai covenant. Yahweh had promised to come to the people's defense as their covenant God. But instead of waiting for His protection, they took matters into their own hands and made defense agreements with the nations. By this action they cast off their greatest security and provoked a judgment as bitter as the hemlock found in their fields (10:4b).

Israel had increased her sinning with the years. She had, Hosea charged, outdone the wickedness at Gibeah (9:9). She had missed the mark which Yahweh had set for her. As a result of that failure, she forsook Him. By that action she cast off all that was good and compromised herself to the point that she had now begun to look like those whom she loved. She had been remade in the image of her lovers.

3. *Israel Remade in the Image of Her Lovers* (9:10, 13). The relationship between Israel and Yahweh was to have been one of intimacy and affection. It was, as we have already seen, comparable to marriage — a relationship of love and concern. Like all such relationships, the parties are affected by each other. They usually act alike and respond favorably to the desires and wishes of the one they love. In fact, they may develop similar tastes; they may walk, stand, or sit alike. One may even adopt the habits of the other. Since this is often the case, and there seem to be many examples to support the possibility, Hosea sought to make a point of this as an illustration of the situation as he found it in Israel.

In 9:10, the prophet charged Israel with having become ". . . like that which they loved." The nation, having consecrated herself to the worship of Baal, or to shame as at Baal-peor, had become like the ones she loved and served. That is, since the Baalim were abominable to Yahweh, and since Israel had become like them, she had in a sense become as abominable as the gods she worshiped. The nation took on the likeness, even the character, of those she "loved" and worshiped. It was a solemn truth in Hosea's day, and it is now, that men tend to become like that which they love. This being so, Hosea could affirm the fact that Israel had been "remade in the image of her lovers."

But there was more to it than that Israel would become like those she loved — the Baalim. She would also suffer as those committed to Baal. That is, she would suffer like the citizens of Tyre, the home of the Baalim, who had lost their offspring to the sword of the invader (9:13). So would Israel lose hers. In other words, having become like their lovers (the Baalim), they would also suffer the fate of those who were totally committed to the Baalim.

One can sense the ominousness of Israel's situation. The day of judgment was at hand — days of visitation, days of recompense.

4. *The Days of Visitation, the Days of Recompense* (9:2-7a, 11, 16-17; 10:2b, 5-8, 10-11, 14-15). Yahweh determined that the days of Israel's afflictions were to be filled with various kinds of judgment. For one thing, the people's sustenance, which in verse 2 was represented by the wine vat and the threshing floor, would not be forthcoming because they would be denied these resources (9:3). They would be taken from "Jehovah's land" (Israel) and returned to a bondage like that which they had experienced in Egypt. In this new bondage their drink offering would no longer be made. Neither would their sacrifices be acceptable (9:4). In fact, their bread would be "the bread of mourners." "The bread of mourners" was the designation given the food which those in mourning ate. This involved the food consumed during the traditional period of seven days (Deut. 24:14) of mourning. It may even have been a reference to the meals eaten at the time of a funeral.

Another approach to the problem of "the bread of mourners" could be that in ancient Israel any person who came into the presence of one who was deceased was automatically considered unclean for a given period of time (Num. 19:14). Not only was the person considered unclean, but anything touched by such a person was thereby made unclean (Num. 19:22). Therefore, the food prepared by one who had been in the presence of death was made unclean by the touch of one preparing it. Not only that, but any person consuming food which had been prepared by an unclean person was made unclean by simply touching it.

Now, since Israel was facing another exile, the offerings, including a portion of their food, could not be made at the sanctuary. Offerings could not be brought under those conditions. They would be unclean, therefore, because they would have been offered in a foreign ("unclean") land. On the basis of this, the bread, which they offered in part as a sacrifice, was referred to as "the bread of mourners." That is, it was unclean bread which could not be offered to Yahweh. It could only serve to satisfy "their appetite" (9:4b). It would not be permitted to serve the dual purpose of being an acceptable sacrifice and an acceptable food at the same time, as it had while they were still in the land. The making of sacrifices would no longer be possible for them, as a matter of fact (9:5). In addition, their objects of pride ("pleasant thing of silver"), that is, their richly and elegantly furnished dwellings, would be given over to the "nettles" and "thorns." Their treasures would be left to the erosive force of the elements in nature.

With Israel in Egypt and her treasures left to destruction, the glory of the nation would disappear with the swiftness of a bird in flight (9:11*a*). Yet, lest one misunderstand the implications involved, more than material glory would be affected. The people's own glory would be affected as they were denied the anticipated glory of their offspring (9:11*b*-12, 16). For all practical purposes, they would not become the glorious people of Yahweh's elective race, they would be no more than castaways — "wanderers among the nations" — and by their own choice at that, a choice which they had made by refusing to heed Yahweh (9:17).

Having lost their material and personal glory, Israel had but one other possible avenue of glory: the religious. Yet, even here they made the wrong choices. They turned to the gods of the nations and adopted their customs and practices rather than turning to Yahweh and those avenues of service and worship required by Him. As a consequence, the altars and idols used in these corrupt practices would be destroyed or taken away as trophies of war (10:2*b*, 5-7), and the high places where they had gathered for their compromised religious activity would be a abandoned. They would be left to the thorns and thistles (5:8).

These stark conditions would be established in due time and they would come about because of "their two transgressions" (10:10). The nation had forsaken Yahweh for other gods, and/or they had set up kings but not as He willed (see 8:4). Therefore, Yahweh would no longer give them the pleasant task of treading out the grain, a task which would provide them with all that they desired or needed for food. Instead, he would assign them the hard and painful tasks of pulling a cart, or plowing and breaking up the soil in preparation for the sowing of seed (10:11). In other words, Israel's state would change. They would no longer have tasks which they would delight in. Instead they would be assigned tasks that were difficult and painful. These things would be so because they had forsaken Yahweh and had placed their confidence in false gods or in their own plans.

Difficult and painful tasks would not be the total punishment, however. The people would be devastated by their enemies (10:14*b*). This destruction would be as total as that at Beth-arbel (no doubt a famous battle known to Hosea and his hearers, but lost to history), in which women and children, usually spared in warfare, were mercilessly slaughtered (10:14*b*). Bethel, the religious center of Israel identified with the nation, would be annihilated, and the monarchy would be cut off (10:15). Israel, who had become what she was because of what Yahweh had done for her, had rejected Him and His purpose. In His stead she gave herself to her own devices and the gods of the nations. She could, therefore, expect the judgment of Yahweh. If ever there had been a time for Israel to seek the mercy of Yahweh, that time had come.

5. *Time to Seek Yahweh* (10:12). Time was fast running out for Israel — and Judah, too. The nation had sought security and plenty in the gods of the nations and in the treaties which they had negotiated with the nations, but to no avail. Now, their only hope was to turn to Yahweh. This the prophet entreated them to do. To demonstrate their repentance they must sow in righteousness and reap in kindness. This would be an entirely new approach for them, however. Their old practices would have to be broken up, as one would plow a field. Then they would be able to sow righteousness and reap kindness. In other words, a total transformation must take place. The old compacted soil of Israel's heart would have to be pulverized. After that, they would be able to realize the noble goals of righteousness and kindness set for them by Yahweh. But the breaking was a thing which could only be accomplished by their turning to Yahweh. If they could find it in their hearts to "seek Yahweh" in the intimacy and fullness of love and obedience, He would respond to their seeking. Then, Israel would have become the recipients of His righteousness, they would have learned their own responsibility in righteousness and would give themselves to the performance of it. Afterward, the charge of having forgotten their Maker would be dropped. They would then be known as a people of righteousness and kindness — characteristics which should have been manifest in their lives since the days of Sinai.

FOR FURTHER STUDY

1. Read the article on "Calf, Golden" found in IDB, Vol. I, pp. 488-9, and the one on "Calf Worship" in ZPBD, p. 141.
2. Read the article on "Peor" in IDB, Vol. III, p. 728, and ZPBD, p. 635.
3. Does your society tend to forget who God is and what He has done for it? How is this evident? Discuss.
4. Has your nation made choices which involved casting off the good for that which was harmful? List some of those. How have they affected your own community? What can be done to encourage a new direction? Discuss.
5. Do you believe that men generally tend to become like those they love? Have you? How have you been affected by a love affair? Is the

principle of becoming like the one whom you love a New Testament principle? If so, wherein is it reflected?

6. Do you believe that time may be running out for your country? If so, what would you say to it? Have you said it? If not, why not? Do you believe it would do any good? What good?

CHAPTER 9

LOVE FINDS A WAY
(Hosea 11)

1. Israel's God of Love (11:1)
2. Yahweh's Concern for Israel's Needs (11:3-4)
3. Israel's Rejection of Yahweh's Proffered Grace (11:2)
4. Israel Left to Her Own Choices (11:5-6)
5. The Turning of Yahweh's Heart (11:7-8)
6. Yahweh Is God and Not Man (11:9)
7. Love Never Fails (11:10)

The theme of love is found in varied degrees throughout the Book of Hosea. From the love of the prophet, which was the basis of his purchase of Gomer, to Yahweh's love for Israel, as reflected in one divine expression after another, the theme occurs. Chapter 11 is the high-water mark of this emphasis.

1. *Israel's God of Love* (11:1). Hosea began the message of chapter 11 with the declaration that the motivation for Yahweh's calling Israel ("when . . . a child") out of Egypt was love (11:1). Though some may relate this action solely to Israel's deliverance from bondage, it probably should be extended to include the kindness of Yahweh expressed through the making of the covenant. The warmth of feeling expressed in that action was the kind that one would expect to see expressed by a father toward his favorite child.

Israel, who corresponded to a favored child of Yahweh, had been the recipient of great affection initially. Later, when she turned from Yahweh, she was no longer considered by Him to be His, and was no longer treated as such. It has been suggested that these words were a polemic, in part at least, to call attention to the contrast between Israel's present relationship (of not being His) and the one which existed at the time of the Exodus. If so, it has been most effectively done. Things had changed considerably. The change provoked Yahweh's increased concern for, and interest in, Israel's needs.

2. *Yahweh's Concern for Israel's Needs* (11:3-4). The warm and loving relationship between Yahweh and Israel resulted in Yahweh's

continuing concern for Israel's every need. This concern reached back to the time of the nation's infancy, to the time when Yahweh taught her to walk (11:3a). The "infant" Israel needed to learn to walk responsibly. That is, the nation in her youth, while so open and vulnerable to those who would lead her astray, needed to be taught by Yahweh so that she might choose the right paths. Yahweh attempted to do this by giving Israel the law and the prophets.

Teaching one to walk, as Yahweh taught Israel, involves more than a knowledge of the right way, however. It demands the patience to wait for the child to rest after he has grown weary, and it requires a sensitivity to the child's hurt, as well as a willingness to bind up his scratches and bruises. Yahweh had been willing to respond in these ways to Israel's needs. When she had grown tired, or after she had fallen and hurt herself in the process of learning to walk, He had taken her up in His arms. He had bound up her wounds and/or held her securely until she was rested and healed (11:3b).

Yahweh had not only taught Israel to walk and cared for her when she was hurt, but He had drawn her with "bands of love" (11:4). Here, in addition to the figure of a father's care, reflected in verse 3, Hosea adds the analogy of the teamster. He declared that Yahweh had drawn ("drew") Israel with "bands of love" instead of driving her along with a whip (11:4a). Hosea meant that the people had been led (encouraged and gently led along) by one who had been patient and understanding, rather than by one who was impatient and abusive. Yahweh had helped them bear the burden ("lift up the yoke on their jaws") rather than adding to it. Their God had set food before them rather than forcing them to continue without proper nourishment (11:4b).

Thus, Yahweh had cared for Israel. As He did so, He manifested His great concern for her needs and made a commitment to meet them.

Israel would have been expected to respond positively to such expressions of concern and care, but she did not. She, in fact, rejected Yahweh's proffered grace.

3. *Israel's Rejection of Yahweh's Proffered Grace* (11:2). Instead of responding to the love and care of Yahweh, Israel rejected these. By doing so, she in reality rejected Yahweh and in that way manifested an unbelievable lack of gratitude. Yahweh had expressed His love toward the nation in delivering her out of Egypt. One would have expected that Israel would have been faithful to Him on that account, if for no other, but not so. The people had, instead, turned from Him. They had sacrificed to the Baalim and had burned incense

to their idols. But Yahweh had not treated them as they deserved. He would have been justified, had He chosen to do so, in delivering them up to an early judgment. Instead, He sent the prophets to call them to return to Him (11:2). But this preaching did not accomplish what He had intended; it but increased the people's obstinacy. The more the prophets preached, the more adamant the people became. They were all the more determined to commit their allegiance to those who in reality had been unable to provide them with anything at all.

Thus, Israel spurned the additional grace which Yahweh extended them in sending the prophets to call them to repentance. Instead of responding to His will, they chose to go their own way. Because they did so, He granted them what they wanted. He left them to their own choices.

4. *Israel Left to Her Own Choices* (11:5-6). The people of Israel had been determined to depart from Yahweh; they were insistent upon the Baalim and the graven images. So, by responsibility of choice, they had to be willing to bear the consequences. Their choice of the gods of the pagan world suggested their preference for the world which those gods provided. They wanted to live under the sovereignty of pagan gods rather than Yahweh's. They wanted to live in a pagan world. Since Israel was Yahweh's, however, they could not remain in His land and be His people while they served other gods. If they continued to insist upon doing so, there was but one way open to them. They would have to be put out of the land. They would be placed in those lands who acknowledged gods other than Yahweh. Since this was what Israel wanted, Yahweh would grant it. They would be returned to a land where they would be subjected to the supposed sovereignty and rule of other gods (11:5).

These conditions of enslavement and domination would be the end result of Israel's defeat by her enemies (11:6). Israel's defenses ("bars") would be inadequate, and her plans ("counsels") would but contribute to her undoing. Israel, left to her own choices, would be a nation of defenseless and helpless people.

Though Yahweh temporarily left Israel to her choices, and their attendant consequences, it was not something in which He found satisfaction. To the contrary, it brought Him distress and pain. His heart turned within Him.

5. *The Turning of Yahweh's Heart* (11:7-8). Israel, in spite of the goodness of Yahweh, had insisted upon rebelling ("backsliding") against Him (11:7). Their rebellious spirit brought the nation to the verge of destruction. Yahweh had determined to hand them over to

their enemies, as previously indicated. But just as this doom was about to come to pass, just as the judgment was about to fall, Yahweh's heart convulsed with pain over the possibility of giving Israel up (11:8). The very thought of Yahweh's casting off His bride (Israel) aroused His compassion to such an extent He could no longer tolerate the idea of her destruction. He could not treat her as Admah and Zeboim had been treated when Sodom and Gomorrah were destroyed. Yet, simple justice would require some action.

How could Israel be spared if others, guilty of no more, had been destroyed? The only way it could be done would be through some divine intervention, some supernatural determination. The very love of Yahweh for Israel would find a way. His mercy would somehow contravene the demand for justice. And He could do this because He was God and not man.

6. *Yahweh Is God and Not Man* (11:9). Though sparing Israel might appear to have been impossible for men, for Yahweh it was not only possible, but an overwhelming desire. How could that be? Because of the very nature of Yahweh: He was "God and not man" (11:9). That fact made it possible for him to act, as the sovereign God, in the best interest of His own purpose in history.

That purpose, as He determined it, was to spare at least a portion of Israel. He would not completely destroy the nation. He could not do so and remain true to His commitment to Abraham, that the world would be blessed through him and his seed. Having once committed Himself unconditionally, Yahweh would insist upon carrying out His intention. He would do so, in spite of the nation's failure, through His unfailing love. He would judge the nation, yes, but He would spare a remnant. Love, divine love, never fails.

7. *Love Never Fails* (11:10). Though Israel would be brought under divine judgment and sent off into exile, that would not mean the end of Yahweh's purpose for His people. He would call to them ("roar to them"), and they would respond trembling with fear from their places of captivity (11:10). Like frightened ("trembling") birds they would return to their homeland (11:11). Love had found a way. It always had. Israel, though punished for her sins, would not be annihilated. Some would be spared, because Yahweh was divine and not human. His justice was tempered with love, and in the end He would work His purpose through those who would be spared. It is like that with love — it is always like that when it is divine love. It finds a way.

70

FOR FURTHER STUDY

1. Read the article on "Love in the Old Testament" in IDB, Vol. III, pp. 164-168, and the article on "Love" in ZPBD, pp. 493-4.
2. Read the articles on "Admah" in IDB, Vol. I, p. 46, and on "Zeboim" in IDB, Vol. IV, p. 940.
3. Does Hosea advance the concept of Yahweh's love? Wherein? What added dimension do you see reflected in his teaching? Discuss.
4. Does God have the right as Sovereign to contravene the laws of justice? Has He done so? How does the Old Testament deal with this matter? The New Testament? Discuss.
5. In what way did the love of God finally express itself to Israel? Did that expression create a problem for man's sense of justice? How? How have you dealt with it?
6. What does Hosea reveal about God as a person? What characteristics are reflected in chapter 11? Discuss.

CHAPTER 10

WHEN THE OPTIONS BECOME OBVIOUS
(Hosea 12, 13)

1. A Look at the Past — The Way It Used to Be (12:3-4, 9-10, 13; 13:1, 5-6)
2. A Look at the Present — The Way Things Were (12:1, 7-8a, 11; 13:1b-2, 6, 9, 16)
3. A Look at the Potential — The Way It Might Have Been (13:4)
4. A Look at the Probable — The Way It Would Be (12:1, 8b-9, 14; 13:3, 12b, 14-15)
5. A Look at Grace — The Way It Could Still Be (12:6)

In this section (chapters 12-13), Hosea drew a contrast between the way things used to be in Israel, the way they were, and the way they should have been. Since the Israelites had not given themselves to making the most of their relationship with Yahweh, the prophet sought to focus their attention upon the options. They could either suffer the judgment of Yahweh for their failure, or they could turn to Him in repentance. By making the options so obvious, the prophet was attempting to nudge Israel to choose the way that would lead to their salvation. He began by looking at the way things used to be.

1. *A Look at the Past – The Way It Used to Be* (12:3-4, 9-10, 13; 13:1, 5-6). By turning to the past, a time when relations between Yahweh and Israel were considered to have been ideal, Hosea was establishing a norm. This norm was to have served as the standard for the nation through the years.

The first reference to the past is found in 12:3-4. Here, Hosea referred to the activities in which Jacob had engaged so that he might become the beneficiary of his brother's blessings. Without noting the reprehensibleness of Jacob's plotting, Hosea focused attention upon his desire to precede his brother Esau in birth so that he might be the recipient of the rights and privileges which would otherwise go to his brother. In this particular case, Jacob's aspiration was presented as desirable. That is, it was considered noble to aspire to the position of first-born (12:3a). The reference to Jacob's wrestling with the angel

(Gen. 32:22ff.) was also interpreted as being worthy because it was shown to be an attempt to gain the favor of Yahweh (12:5b). After all, as a result of Jacob's striving, Yahweh had revealed Himself and had spoken to him (12:4).

By suggesting that Jacob's conduct was, in one way, worthy of emulation, the prophet was establishing a norm for Jacob's descendants (Israel). Hosea was, by implication at least, suggesting that Israel should follow the "example" of Jacob if they wished to be blessed of Yahweh.

In verse 9 of chapter 12, Hosea made another appeal to the past. This time he referred to Yahweh's help at the time of the Exodus and, by implication, his willingness to help at the present. The norm, then, was to look to Yahweh at the present as they had in the past.

In addition, the people of Israel were reminded of Yahweh's special favor as seen in His sending the prophets to warn them of impending judgments (12:10). This had been Yahweh's way in the past. It was His norm for the present. To heed the prophet would result in a continued relationship of good-will and blessing. It had worked in the past; it could work in the present. In fact, Hosea attributed Israel's deliverance from Egypt to a prophet (Moses) (12:13). Was he not suggesting that by heeding the call of the prophet's preaching, they would be delivered from the threat of bondage?

Still another effort by Hosea to establish the normative is found in 13:1. Though the verse has been variously interpreted, the most probable explanation is that it refers to the "trembling" response of Israel when Yahweh first called to her and when she made her initial response (see 2:15). She responded, or at least her leaders responded, in "trembling" — in awe and humility. If this was the point of reference, the prophet was trying to get the nation to reestablish the norm of the past as the preferred norm for the present. If they did, they would once more be exalted as they had been in the past (13:1).

One last look at the past is seen in 13:5-6. As a result of Israel's response in "trembling," Yahweh is depicted as having cared for her through the wilderness wanderings and granting her plenty as long as she continued to follow Him in faithfulness. Hosea was making the point that the norm for becoming the recipients of Yahweh's faithfulness was that of humility and trust.

By looking to the past and using Israel's responses in that phase of her existence as the norm, Hosea was, by implication at least, calling the nation back to the ideals of that past. In doing so, he was establishing these ideals as one of the options open to them.

73

2. *A Look at the Present – The Way Things Were* (12:1, 7-8*a*, 11; 13:1*b*-2, 6, 9, 16). Conditions in Israel during the ministry of Hosea were far from normal, if indeed Israel's earlier condition could have been considered normal. At the present, Israel carried out acts of violence ("desolation"), falsehood ("lies"), and demonstrated a lack of trust in Yahweh. These had turned Israel in the direction of Egypt and Assyria for protection. She had turned from the norm and had, thereby, jeopardized her future, her life (12:1).

In addition to the conditions described in 12:1, the Israelites were charged with being as dishonest and fraudulent in their dealings with their fellowmen as the Canaanites ("traffiker") had been, and then of boasting of their gain from such reprehensible practices (12:8*a*). How far they had drifted from the moorings of their youth, at which time they had dealt honestly and humbly with their fellowman as well as with their God. They had drifted so far, in fact, that Gilead, standing for Israel as a whole, was described as being morally bankrupt. Because the people had permitted this to happen, they, along with their places of worship, would be destroyed (12:11).

As reflected in 13:1, Israel's practices, rather than exalting the nation, would bring it to its end. These words of warning went unheeded, however. The people but multiplied their idols and poured out their affection ("kiss the calves") upon them (13:2). This apostasy placed the nation in peril. Divine judgment would inevitably overtake a people so open to compromise.

The wickedness throughout the land was one more evidence Israel had forgotten Yahweh (13:6*b*). Not only had they forgotten He was the source of all their blessings; they also had forgotten He was the God of judgment (13:9). As a result, Israel had, as it were, destroyed herself. She had forsaken Yahweh, her only source of help. By doing so, she had forsaken life itself. As a result of her forgetting, yea, even rebelling against Yahweh, God would subject her to the cruelty and the atrocities of her enemies (13:16). The future had been cancelled. Tomorrow had been lost.

How far from the norm the picture now described by the prophet! Israel had forsaken, forgotten, and even rebelled against Yahweh. What a different picture the present in Israel provided! And this tragedy is but accentuated when Israel's initial potential is considered.

3. *A Look at the Potential – The Way It Might Have Been* (13:4). Yahweh had proved Himself as Israel's deliverer from Egypt, had commanded His people to have no other god, and had declared Himself to be their only savior. The nation should then have had

every reason to believe He would be their help in the future (13:4). In other words, Israel had a potential no other nation had ever had. They were to have been the means by which Yahweh would bless all of the nations of earth (see Gen. 12:1ff.). With this as His primary intent, Yahweh had led Israel out of Egypt even in the face of staggering odds. He had given them the commandments to guide them. And, as if that were not enough, He had promised to fight on their behalf in the face of all of their enemies (compare Deut. 4:1ff.; 7:17ff.).

Because of what Yahweh had done for Israel, and in view of all He had promised to do through her, the nation's potential for good was obvious. Yahweh had committed Himself to bless the entire world through Israel. That He did, but not through corporate Israel. It was accomplished through one out of Israel — the Messiah!

Since the nation, as such, had failed to measure up to Yahweh's expectations, they would suffer the judgment they deserved. The future would be filled with defeat and suffering.

4. *A Look at the Probable – The Way It Would Be* (12:2, 8*b*-9, 14; 13:3, 12*b*, 14-15). Since the nation had not reached its potential, the probability of Yahweh's judgment seemed certain. Yahweh would recompense the nation in accordance with its doings (12:1). That is, they would reap according to what they had sown. Although they would deny dishonesty in their dealings, all that they had gained would not expiate the guilt they had brought upon themselves by their shameful deeds (12:8). Instead, they would be driven from their abundance and security out into another wilderness, where they would live in tents while they wandered through the endless desert, as they had in days gone by (12:9), and all of this would happen as a result of their having provoked Yahweh to anger (12:14).

The nation, as a result of these conditions, was so insecure that it was characterized as being as transitory as a "morning cloud," as the "dew that passeth early away," as "the chaff that is driven with the whirlwind out of the threshing floor," as the smoke which so quickly vanishes when blown about by the wind (13:3).

There was no way for the Israelites to escape divine judgment. Though they might act innocent, Yahweh knew that they were guilty. In fact, He had collected ("bound up") their iniquity and was holding their sin "in store" (13:12). Nothing had been forgotten. All of their sins were to be called to account. Yahweh had not missed one evil deed. In due time, He would encourage Sheol to do its worst by them (13:14*a*). He would show them no mercy (13:14*b*). Whatever their former state, and it had been one of prosperity and plenty (13:15*a*), their future would be one of drought, famine, and loss — loss of every valuable gained through their dishonesty and falsehood (13:15b).

Samaria, standing for all of Israel, would "bear her guilt" ("become desolate"); and suffer the most inhumane atrocities imaginable (13:16).

What dreadful portents the future held for Israel! The nation, having failed to take the way of faithfulness, had chosen the way of wickedness. That choice had eliminated the other option. They were, by all that appeared to be just, doomed to destruction. Were all other options lost? The answer to that question was the key to Israel's future, as well as the future of all mankind.

5. *A Look at Grace – The Way It Could Still Be* (12:6). In verses 3 and 4 of chapter 12, Hosea, reflecting upon the way things used to be, set a context for the way things might still become. Since Yahweh had responded to the aspirations of Jacob, surely He could and would respond in mercy to all who looked to Him in repentance and faith. Therefore, Hosea called upon the nation to "turn" to Yahweh (12:6). The alternative to judgment was, and had always been, a turning to Yahweh. Evidence that they had turned to Him would be the exercise of justice in all areas of life, the manifestation of kindness (mercy) in their interpersonal relationships, and faith in Yahweh rather than in idols and neighboring nations (12:6b).

The people of Israel, by their own choice, had rejected the option to do the will of Yahweh which was open to them, as it had been to their fathers. The options open to the Israelites now were judgment and grace. They must choose the one or the other. With the options so obvious, Hosea encouraged them to turn to Yahweh who would respond in grace, but they would not. Had they done so, the course of history would have been quite different.

FOR FURTHER STUDY

1. Read the articles on "Jacob" in IDB, Vol. II, pp. 782-787, and in ZPBD, pp. 398-399
2. Read the article on "Canaanites" in IDB, Vol. I, pp. 494-498, and the article on "Canaan, Canaanites" in ZPBD, p. 143.
3. Do you see a parallel between the situation in Israel during Hosea's ministry and the present situation in your own country? If so, what does it suggest? Discuss.
4. Do you tend to idealize the past? How? Why? Is it a valid thing to do? If so, why so? If not, why not?

5. Should a nation consider itself favored if there is a strong prophetic element in it? Why? Discuss.
6. Have there been any changes in the options presented by Hosea? Why not? Discuss.
7. In light of the options enunciated by Hosea, what should you do? Discuss.

CHAPTER 11

THE EFFECT OF GENUINE REPENTANCE
(Hosea 14)

1. The Need for Repentance (14:1, 4, 9)
2. The Attitude of Genuine Repentance (14:2-4)
3. The Effect of Genuine Repentance (14:5-9)

A large part of Hosea's ministry was spent condemning the nation for its sin. Since he and the other eighth-century prophets put so much of their emphasis here, some have suggested that these prophets were totally concerned with judgment. As a consequence, many have questioned the passages of hope which appear in the prophetic messages, suggesting that they were added sometime later.

This approach to the "hope passages" has been challenged, however, by those who believe that every true prophet would have preached hope as well as judgment. There seems to be sufficient evidence from the prophets to support this claim. Every canonical prophetic book contains both aspects; they contain messages of judgment followed by messages of hope. In fact, this seems to be a persistent pattern in all biblical preaching. Words of warning followed by the proffered grace of God — this has always been the biblical way. In the light of this fact, there may be considerably less reason to question the hope passages in Hosea than may at first appear.

Chapter 14, a section on hope, follows in general the hope passages found in various places throughout chapters 11-13. There is first a declaration of the need for repentance.

1. *The Need for Repentance* (14:1, 4, 9). This section of Hosea's prophecy opens with an exhortation calling the nation back to Yahweh (14:1a). This repeated emphasis makes it clear that Israel has persisted in her refusal to turn to Him. She had insisted upon continuing in her apostasy and had fallen (been overwhelmed by disaster) as a result of her iniquity (14:1b).

In verse 4, the prophet turned to Israel's continual backsliding.

He called attention to the fact that the people had abandoned the faith they had once held. In having done so, they had brought great harm upon the nation. This pointed up the need for repentance, the need for returning to Yahweh.

This need is also implied in the last verse of the book, where the warning that transgressors would "fall" (stumble) is found. These (the transgressors) defied the known will and purpose of Yahweh and passed beyond the limits fixed by Him. In this particular case, the "limit" referred to was the one set by the law. It set the boundary for Israel in relation to Yahweh and in relation to their fellowman.

These practices — apostasy, iniquity, backsliding, and transgression — clearly pointed to a need for repentance. That obvious need was now the primary factor in Hosea's ministry. The repentance which Hosea sought was not the traditional kind, however. It was not to be another attempt to buy Yahweh's favor through ritual activity (see 6:1ff.). The repentance which Hosea called for was to be genuine and heart-felt. It was to be a true expression of the person's (or the nation's) deepest being.

2. *The Attitude of Genuine Repentance* (14:2-4). The repentance called for by Hosea was the genuine expression of a contrite heart. The penitent could never receive forgiveness as long as there was a contradiction between what he did in an act of repentance and what was truly in his heart. Therefore, Hosea called upon Israel to leave off the empty ritual and to take up "words" (prayers) reflecting a genuine repentance which was the only basis of forgiveness (14:2a).

These "words" must include, among other things, the confession of iniquity. That is, the prayer must reflect the honest acknowledgment that they were guilty of crooked and perverse methods in their dealings with others, and thus with Yahweh (14:2b).

These "words" were also to include the confession that they had misplaced their faith by turning to Assyria and by putting their confidence in the idols they had created with their own hands (14:3).

Though it was required that these "words" be genuine, words alone would not suffice. There was a prior consideration. There must be a knowledge of, and confidence in, the goodness of Yahweh and His ability to forgive their sins. Such a confidence is reflected in the suggested prayer of Hosea, where he instructed the people to call upon Yahweh if they wished to be rid of iniquity (14:2b).

Not only must there be an acknowledgment of Yahweh's ability to remove sin, but a claim upon His mercy must be made (14:3c). He must be recognized as the one who responds, not as expected or deserved, but as unexpected and undeserved. Israel had no merit to claim; therefore anything done for her would have to be undeserved — unmerited.

A third awareness was necessary if Israel was to reflect an attitude of genuine repentance. The people must recognize Yahweh's love and cast themselves upon it (14:4a), because it was the ultimate basis of Yahweh's forgiveness. After the Israelites had confessed their sin and acknowledged Yahweh's power, mercy, and love, they were in position to ask His forgiveness ("say unto . . .") (14:2). To ask forgiveness would provoke His mercy; and His mercy, and that alone, would provide forgiveness for those in sin (14:4c).

3. *The Effect of Genuine Repentance* (14:5-9). The forgiveness gained through genuine repentance would have lasting effects upon the nation. Hosea called Israel's attention to some of these.

First, in verse 4, Hosea had reminded the people that Yahweh would "heal their backsliding." That is, He would cure them of backsliding; or it could mean He would heal the harm brought upon them on account of their backsliding. Either, or both, may have been the intent of the passage. In either case, the tragic effects of backsliding would be forgiven (be healed) in response to genuine repentance.

As a result of their repentance and their changed attitude, Yahweh's anger would be turned away from them (14:4b). He would love them freely. That is, He would respond to their repentant attitude in love rather than in anger. Repentance was what was required — genuine repentance. This would be reflected in their ritual activity, to be sure, but it would be more than that. There must be a genuine attitude on their part. Yahweh's love could not be bought by ritual activity. It could only be experienced through the grace which was Yahweh's response to genuine repentance.

With their backsliding healed, Yahweh's anger turned away, and His love now directed toward them, Israel would embark upon an era of prosperity, security, and service.

Since all his hearers knew that dew was the primary source of moisture for the crops in Israel from late spring to late fall, Yahweh referred to Himself as dew (14:5). As a result of their new relationship, Yahweh would be as meaningful to them as dew to their crops during the hot, dry summer months.

In light of Yahweh's faithfulness, the nation could expect to become as lovely and profuse, in spiritual and material ways, as the lilies were in natural ways. They would be as secure against any and every onslaught, as the deep-rooted trees on Lebanon were against the drought, or any other form of devastation (14:5-6). Those dwelling in Israel ("under his shadow") would be most successful in their planting and harvesting. They would be as pleasant an odor to Yahweh as the smell of the wine was to the owner of the vineyard (14:7).

After the blessings of repentance had been placed in full view by the prophet, the nation, speaking with itself, asked, "What have I to do any more with idols?" (14:8). It was as though the people were suggesting that, in light of the blessings of repentance, "we will never turn to idols again." The reasons were, first, because they (the idols) had failed them, and second, because of all Yahweh could and would mean to them. In light of the failure of the idols and the promises of Yahweh, the wise, prudent, and just would walk in His ways and live. But transgressors would fall therein and be destroyed (14:9).

Thus, in the closing chapter of the book, Hosea was used of Yahweh to call attention to Israel's greatest need — repentance. He also reminded them of the effects of repentance that was genuine. In doing so, Hosea served his day well. And he has served every generation since, because the results of repentance in Hosea's day are the results of repentance in our own day. Therefore, the word of the prophet to our own day would be, repent! Those doing so can expect forgiveness and the abundance of His grace. Those refusing will live out their lives in sin and the spiritual poverty which it always brings.

FOR FURTHER STUDY

1. Read the articles on "Repentance" in IDB, Vol. IV, pp. 33-34; and in ZPBD, pp. 711-712.
2. Read the article on "Apostasy" in IDB, Vol. I, p. 170; and in ZPBD, p. 52.
3. Are men still guilty of the sins found in chapter 14? How do they express themselves, if so? Discuss.
4. What message would you address to your day in light of man's sins? How would you use Hosea in what you would say? Discuss.
5. What results have you experienced from your own repentance? Has your repentance always been genuine? What is true repentance? Discuss.
6. Compare your experience of grace with that of a friend. What similarities are there? What differences, if any? Discuss.